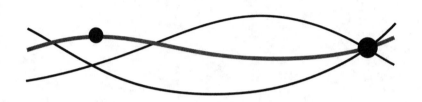

MICAH, NAHUM, HABAKKUK, AND ZEPHANIAH

MESSAGES OF JUSTICE AND RENEWAL

Micah, Nahum, Habakkuk, and Zephaniah

Messages of Justice and Renewal

F. Wayne Mac Leod

Authentic
MEDIA

Copyright © 2004 by F. Wayne Mac Leod

00 09 08 07 06 05 04   7 6 5 4 3 2 1
Published by Authentic Media
129 Mobilization Drive, Waynesboro, GA 30830 USA authenticusa@stl.org
and 9 Holdom Avenue, Bletchley, Milton Keynes, Bucks, MK1 1QR, UK

ISBN: 1-932805-02-8

Unless otherwise noted, all Scripture is taken from the HOLY BIBLE, NEW
INTERNATIONAL VERSION ®. Copyright © 1973, 1978, 1984 by International Bible
Society. Used by permission of Zondervan Publishing House. All rights reserved.

All rights reserved. No part of this book may be reproduced in any form without
permission in writing from the publisher, except in the case of brief quotations embodied
in critical articles or reviews.

Cover design: Paul Lewis

Contents

Habakkuk

Zephaniah

Preface

In this commentary, we will meet four prophets. We will hear how Micah exhorted a people whose materialism and greed had stripped them of a sense of their need for God. We will meet the prophet Nahum who encouraged God's people by proclaiming victory over the enemies that had conquered them because of their sin and rebellion. We will see how Habakkuk struggled with questions of evil and justice. We will observe how Zephaniah spoke to his people about a great renewal and cleansing in the land. Though God's people had turned from him, Zephaniah reassured them of God's delight in them as a people.

My prayer is that this commentary will bring the words of these inspired prophets to our present day and culture. As with the other commentaries in this series, this book is not designed to be intellectual and scholarly but devotional in nature. It is my belief that the message of these prophets is for us today. My hope and prayer is that as you read this commentary the message of these prophets will be clear and simple. I trust that the Lord will use this commentary to draw each reader closer to himself.

I encourage you to take your time reading this commentary. Do not read it in a single sitting. Read the biblical passage and use this commentary to guide you in your reflections on it. Pray over each chapter and ask the Holy Spirit to reveal to you the truth he would have you to see. Take the time to see how these truths apply specifically to your life.

I am so thankful to God for the way he has opened doors for this commentary series to grow. My desire is for the Bible to come alive in this age. I would ask you to pray for me as I continue to write this commentary series. Please pray that as these books go around the world, they would touch many lives by bringing them to the inspired Word of God. God bless you as you read.

Micah

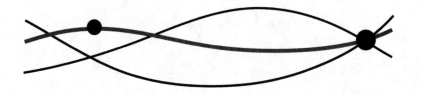

1
Introducing
the Prophet

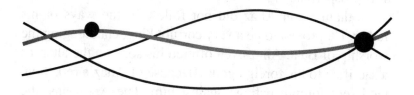

Read Micah 1:1

This is the prophecy of Micah from the village of Moresheth, located in the nation of Judah. While he was from Judah, Micah prophesied to both Israel and Judah. The passage tells us that his words were for Samaria and Jerusalem, the capitals of both nations.

Notice that this prophecy is not of human origin. Verse 1 reminds us that while Micah is the author of the prophecy, the words are the words of the Lord. The prophecy came to Micah by means of a vision. He wrote what he saw. These words are not the reflections of the human author. They are the thoughts and words of God to the nations of Israel and Judah. As we will also see, they are God's words to us as well.

The name Micah means "Who is like the Lord?" This name reflects the uniqueness of God. There is none like him in justice, in love, in holiness, or in power. He is unique in his nature and being.

Verse 1 tells us that Micah prophesied during the reigns of three of Judah's kings: Jotham, Ahaz, and Hezekiah. This not only tells us when Micah prophesied but also gives us a better idea of the times in which he lived.

Under the reign of King Jotham, Judah was militarily quite successful. Jotham walked with the LORD and grew quite powerful and influential. 2 Chronicles 27:5 tells us that Jotham made war with the Ammonites and conquered them. During Jotham's reign, Judah enjoyed the favor of God and was prosperous.

Jotham's son Ahaz did not follow in the ways of his father. He proved to be a very corrupt king, encouraging the worship of Baal. Ahaz even offered his sons on the altar, as a sacrifice to his foreign gods. Because of Ahaz's rebellion, God sent foreign nations against him. The Arameans, the Edomites, and the Philistines all attacked Judah during this time. According to 2 Chronicles 28:5 many inhabitants of Judah were taken captive to Damascus. Ahaz also suffered heavy casualties during a war with Israel (2 Chronicles 28:5–6). As king, he emptied the temple of its furnishings. Some of these furnishings he gave to the Assyrians to enlist their aid against his enemies. He eventually shut the doors of the temple (2 Chronicles 28:24). During the reign of Ahaz, things were radically different from the days of his father, Jotham. Prosperity gave way to oppression and defeat. The worship of the God of Abraham, Isaac, and Jacob gave way to the worship of Baal with all its immorality.

When King Hezekiah came to the throne, a great spiritual renewal took place in the land. The temple doors were reopened and worship reestablished. Prosperity returned to the land and the blessing of God was again evident. In this prosperity, however, Hezekiah's heart became proud. While he did repent of this pride, Scripture reveals that he was very pleased with his achievements and never really did completely conquer his arrogance (2 Chronicles 32:27–31).

The prophet Micah prophesied during all these events. Under Ahaz, Judah was at a low point spiritually. Micah saw Judah moving away from God into horrible rebellion under the reign of Ahaz. The prophet Micah would end his ministry, however, on a more positive note as he saw his people once again return to the LORD under the reign of Hezekiah.

How discouraging it would have been to be a prophet in the days of Ahaz. To watch the nation of Judah move from blessing and prosperity to defeat because of her rebellion against God would not have been easy. The depth of Ahaz's rebellion was in many ways unmatched in the history of Israel. Micah's role, however, was to call God's people back to God. It is my prayer that as you take the time to read this prophecy you will experience that same call.

For Consideration:

• What comfort do you find in the fact that despite the horrible rebellion of his people, God sent Micah to call them back to himself? What does this teach us about God?

• What is your spiritual condition today? Are there any areas of your life where the Lord needs to call you back to himself? What are they?

For Prayer:

• Thank the Lord that he reaches out to us in our sin.

• Do you know someone who is living in rebellion against God? Ask God to call this person back to himself.

• Pray that as you read this book of the Bible you will hear the call of God in your life.

2

Proclamation of Judgment

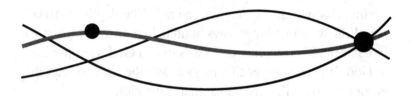

Read Micah 1:2–16

In the opening verses of Micah, the voice of God calls on the earth to listen to what he is about to say. While the judgment that follows is against the towns of Jerusalem and Samaria, the whole earth is to witness the sentencing. Why does God call you and me to hear this judgment? It seems obvious that the Lord has something for us to learn. The judgment is public so that we do not fall into the same trap as Israel and Judah.

Notice that the judgment came from the sovereign Lord in his holy temple. There is only one sovereign Lord. To him one day every knee will bow. He alone has absolute control, right, and power. His decisions cannot be contested or overruled. Even as the temple is holy, so the judgment that comes from that temple is perfect, just, and holy.

In verse 3 the LORD descends from heaven to exercise this judgment on the earth. Notice the scene as he approached. He set his feet on the earth and the mountains melted beneath him. The valleys split apart and melted like wax in the heat of his holy fire. Nothing could stand in his way. His holy judgment consumed the earth.

Why was God so angry? Verse 5 tells us that it is because of the sin of the house of Israel. The cities of Samaria and Jerusalem were guilty before him. These two cities represented the nations of Israel and Judah. In the verses that follow, God pronounces his sentence on the various towns and cities of these two nations.

Samaria (verses 6–7)

Samaria was the capital of Israel. Micah prophesies that it will become a heap of rubble. This once great and prosperous city will become farmland used for planting vines. God will pour stones into the fertile valleys, filling them up so that they will no longer produce crops. The foundations of the city will be leveled to the ground. Her idols, in which she had trusted, will lie broken to pieces in the land. Her false gods will not help her in her hour of need.

Samaria is accused of bringing the wages of a prostitute to the temple. Baal worship of that day involved religious prostitution. Money obtained by this means was finding its way into the temple. In verse 7 God tells Samaria that this money will again be used as the wages of a prostitute. How will this take place? The day is coming when enemies will invade the land and take these treasures. These temple treasures, in the hand of these enemies, will be used to buy the services of prostitutes.

Samaria was guilty before God of hypocrisy. She brought to God her gifts, but they were obtained by impure means. God was interested in the sincerity of the giver. He hated this hypocrisy. God was not fooled by Samaria's outward show of spirituality.

Jerusalem (verses 8–9)

God calls the nation of Judah to wail and moan. The sin of Samaria was incurable (verse 9). It had brought destruction on Samaria. Now like a contagious disease, sin was spreading its poison throughout the land. The corruption had reached the city of Jerusalem. The inhabitants of this city were falling under the influence of Samaria's evil, and they would share in her judgment.

Gath (verse 10)

In verse 10 Micah commands his listeners not to tell of this judgment in Gath. The word *Gath* sounds very much like the Hebrew word "to tell." There may be a play on words here in this verse. Gath was also a city of Philistia, one of the enemies of God's people. If these enemies learned of the plight of Israel, they would very likely seek to take advantage in Israel's moment of weakness. Gath would mock God's people and rejoice in their demise. It may be for this reason that the judgment of God's people is not to be spoken of in the presence of their enemies.

Beth Ophrah (verse 10)

The name *Beth Ophrah* means "house of dust." In this city the inhabitants will literally be rolling in the dust as a sign of mourning because of the judgment of God on them.

Shaphir (verse 11)

Shaphir means "pleasant" or "beautiful." This city will be humbled. She will be stripped of all her beauty and her pleasant land would be filled with shame.

Zaanan (verse 11)

Zaanan means "come out." The inhabitants of this town will not come out. Could this refer to the fact that they would not escape the judgment of God on them?

Beth Ezel (verse 11)

Beth Ezel means "house of taking away." This city is in mourning because its protection was taken away, and they are fully exposed to the wrath and judgment of God.

Maroth (verse 12)

The word *Maroth* sounds very much like the Hebrew word for "bitter." This city writhes in pain because of the great disaster that had come. Her condition is very bitter.

Lachish (verse 13)

The word *lachish* is quite similar to the Hebrew word for "team." This city is called on to harness a team to the chariot. The idea seems to be that the inhabitants are to harness a team and flee from the city because of the great judgment that is coming on the land. God accused this city of being "the beginning of sin to the Daughter of Zion." This city is particularly to be judged because it had led the way in sin and rebellion against God.

Moresheth Gath (verse 14)

Parting gifts will be given to the city of Moresheth Gath. The word *moresheth* resembles the Hebrew word for "betrothed." The imagery here seems to be that of a girl leaving her home after her marriage. Moresheth, like this bride, will have to leave her home.

Aczib (verse 14)

Aczib means "deception." This town will prove to be very deceptive to Israel. We are not told how this will take place. This town will prove to be a stumbling block for the rest of the nation.

Mareshah (verse 15)

Mareshah sounds like the Hebrew word for "conqueror." Because of the sin of these people, God is sending a conqueror against them.

Adullam (verse 15)

In the history of Israel, Adullam was known as the city to which David fled in his flight from the king of Gath (1 Samuel 22:1). The glory of Israel (their rulers) will flee like David to this city as their enemies pursue them.

Micah ends this section by calling the inhabitants of the land to mourn. They are to shave their heads as bald as a vulture as a sign of mourning. They will all be taken away into exile for their sin.

God stands in judgment of his own people. Micah started this section by calling the whole earth to witness this judgment. We are witnesses of this judgment so that we do not repeat the errors of the past.

For Consideration:

- Why is it so hard for us to accept a God who judges sin?

- Why should we be thankful that God will judge sin?

- What are the sins of your nation today?

For Prayer:

- Take a moment to search your own heart. Ask God to reveal any sin that might separate you from him.

- Thank the Lord that he will not allow sin to reign but will one day bring it to light and destroy it.

3

The Sin of Materialism and Greed

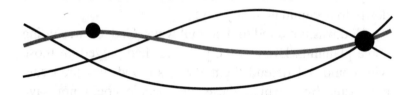

Read Micah 2:1–5

I n the last meditation, we saw how the Lord God brought his judgment on the various cities and towns of Israel and Judah because of their sin. In this section God begins to spell out some of those particular sins. He begins by dealing with the sin of materialism and greed.

Verse 1 introduces us to the rich and powerful people of the land. From this verse, we understand several things about these individuals who were of an evil character. Verse 1 tells us that they lay awake at night, seeking to devise means of enriching themselves. When the morning came, they would carry out their plans because it was in their power to do so. They were powerful individuals. Nothing stopped them from getting what they wanted. They enriched themselves by oppressing the poor. While these rich people had no lack, they still wanted more. The god of materialism is never satisfied. Those who fall prey to his ways can never experience satisfaction. Here we have a picture of the rich losing sleep at night as they plot to obtain more riches for themselves.

Verse 2 tells us that on their beds at night the powerful people in Israel planned how to seize their fellow citizens' houses, fields, and inheritances. Their evil thoughts led them to defraud and seize by force. The god of materialism had captured their hearts. Under his reign, they stooped to any means to satisfy their thirst for wealth and possessions. Their lives revolved around the accumulation of wealth and power. They did not need the wealth, but they were possessed with a desire to accumulate it anyway.

God was not blind to their evil ways. God too was doing some planning. Even as the powerful had preyed on those who could not defend themselves, so God was preparing a disaster from which these evil people could not save themselves. They were a very proud people. Their power and wealth had gone to their heads. The day was coming, however, when they would hang their heads low. People would taunt and ridicule them. The day was coming when the land would mourn because of the condition of the rich and powerful. People would sing about the ruin of the rich and powerful. Their land would be divided. God would take land from the rich and proud and give it to their enemies. Verse 5 tells us that in the end they would have no inheritance at all with the people of God.

The rich and proud felt quite secure. Very likely, they could never have pictured themselves ending up on the scrap heap of life. They would have to learn the hard way that they were not in control of their own destinies. What they had taken years to accumulate, they would lose in a short time. Worse than all this was the fact that they were going to have to face God, whom they had ignored all their lives, and account for their evil deeds.

It is important that we understand that the sin of these people was not in being wealthy or having power. Their sin was their greed and materialism. Greed is not the sin of the rich only but also the sin of the poor and the middle class. Materialism is the sin of letting the things of this world take priority over the Lord and his Word. Greed and materialism can be cruel masters whose thirst for more is never quenched. May God give us grace to resist their pull.

For Consideration:

- God told the materialistic rich that he would strip them of everything they had accumulated. Consider for a moment how quickly we could lose everything we have worked so hard to obtain.

- What is materialism? Why is it so easy to get caught in its trap?

- What is the difference between being rich and being materialistic?

- Discuss how the media uses the human tendencies of greed and materialism to its advantage.

- What does it mean to be content?

For Prayer:

- Ask God to enable you to hold on to your possessions lightly.

- Ask him to give you grace to use what he has given you for his glory.

4

False Prophets

Read Micah 2:6–13

I n the last meditation, we saw how the Lord God accused his people of materialism and greed. He then shifts his attention to the prophets of the land. Listen to what Micah has to say about the prophets who ministered in his day.

Micah opens this section by stating that there were conflicting prophetic messages in the land. There were those prophets who preached that disgrace would come on the people of God because of their sin. Another group of prophets preached a message of peace and prosperity. How were the people of God to make sense out of this confusion? Who was preaching the truth? Even the prophets could not agree.

Does it surprise you that in the days of Micah there was division among spiritual leaders over the Word of God? From the very beginning of time, the enemy has been seeking to twist and distort the Word of God. Even in the

Garden of Eden, Satan sought to cast doubt on this Word. Listen to what he said to Eve: "Did God really say, 'You must not eat from any tree in the garden'?" (Genesis 3:1).

Do you see what Satan was doing? He was trying to cause Eve to doubt the Word of God. By means of careful reason, Satan succeeded in causing her to turn from that Word. Satan told Eve what she wanted to hear. He convinced her to disregard the clear commandment of God and believe lies instead. Eve fell into the trap.

It should not surprise us that Satan is still up to his old tricks. When so many people continue to fall for his lies, there is no need for him to change his tactics. Many years after the incident in the Garden of Eden, Satan is still trying to cast doubt on the truth of the Word of God. Here in the book of Micah, Satan was misleading the prophets. These prophets, in turn, were sharing these false messages with the people of the land and many were deceived.

The false prophets of Micah's day saw it as their duty to comfort the people of the land with false hope. They took a stand against the harsh preaching of doom and gloom and told their listeners that disgrace would not overtake them. Listen to this false reasoning in verse 7: "Should it be said, O house of Jacob: 'Is the Spirit of the LORD angry? Does he do such things?'"

How many times have we heard this argument in our day? What these false prophets were saying was something like this, "Do you really think that God is a God of anger and wrath? What kind of God would leave his people to be disgraced? Is that the type of God we serve?" How many people have been led straight to hell by these half-truths? Countless individuals have believed the lie that God is such a God of love that he would never condemn a sinner. The fact of the matter is that we expect our earthly judges to deal with sin and complain bitterly when they release a criminal onto our streets. When it comes to God, however, we expect him to ignore sin. If we expect our sinful judges to deal harshly with sin and crime, should we not expect a holy God to do the same?

In verse 7 the false prophets tell the people that the words of the Lord do good to those who are upright. The assumption here is that the people were upright. There is a total ignoring of sin in the message of the false prophets. Their goal was to encourage, comfort, and gain followers for themselves. They did this at the expense of truth.

Unlike the false prophets who deceived the people, Micah told things as they were. Micah had serious accusations against his people. Let's examine what he had to say about the people of God.

They Have Risen Up like an Enemy (verse 8)

On the outside the people of God were very religious. They listened to the words of their prophets and practiced the traditions of their ancestors. In reality, however, they were enemies of God. They had rejected his truth and believed the lies of the false prophets. These false prophets were tools in the hands of Satan, giving the people a false hope of eternity and blinding them to the reality of the true Word of God. God's people chose to believe lies and turned their hearts against God and his purposes for them.

They Strip Off the Robe from Those Who Pass By (verse 8)

While they claimed to be God's people, they had no problem stripping off the robes of those who passed by. This imagery could be one of a soldier returning home from a victory. His enemies have been conquered and rendered helpless. As he passes by his enemies, he sees a robe he likes. What does he do? He walks over to his enemy and strips it off him, leaving his enemy humiliated and cold. It is also possible that the people referred to in this verse did this to their own neighbors. These cruel individuals cared nothing for others. Their only concern was for themselves. They took whatever they wanted without respect for the ownership of property.

You Drive Women from Their Homes (verse 9)

In verse 9 Micah states that God's people drove women from their homes and took away the blessing of the children forever. These malicious people thought nothing of taking a home from a poor mother and her children to enrich their own pockets. In taking this home, they also took the only possession this poor mother had to offer to her children as an inheritance.

The false prophets ignored these sins and continued to tell their listeners that God was a God of love. These prophets consoled their audiences with the lie that God would not judge or be angry with them. These misleading words dangerously eased the true guilt of God's people while doing nothing to make them right with God.

In verse 10 Micah, inspired of the Lord, breaks out in prophetic condemnation of these people. "Get up, go away!" he cries. Because of their sin, God's people would be sent from their land. The land had been ruined beyond all remedy by their evil practices. It was defiled. God's people would be cast from his presence. They would understand first-hand that God was indeed a God of wrath and anger—but by then it would be too late.

They Would Believe False Messages of Prosperity (verse 11)

God tells his people through Micah in verse 11 that if a liar and deceiver came prophesying plenty of beer and wine, these people would indeed be ready to listen. God's people were ready to believe anything that appealed to their greed. False prophets have always been popular. They attract masses of people. Their churches are filled, and they are well respected in their communities. Their followers, however, are deceived. They are being led to believe that they are right with God when they are actually headed for eternal separation from God. Don't be deceived. Not every prophet is a true prophet.

God's People Would Be Restored (verses 12–13)

In verse 10 Micah prophesies that God's people would lose their land. Because the land was corrupt, they would be driven from it. In verses 12 and 13 Micah reminds his people that while the judgment of God is real, so is his compassion. God would not forget his people in their exile and bondage. He would gather them together as a shepherd gathers his sheep. God's people would be held in bondage until the day came when a great king would break open the gates and set them free. This great king would pass before them and lead them into triumph. The Lord Jesus is this king. While God's people were set free from their physical bondage in exile under Ezra and Nehemiah, this passage seems to refer to someone greater. The Lord himself would be their deliverer. He would set them free not only from their physical bondage but also from their sin.

It is God's delight to set us free from our sins. This passage clearly tells us that while God is a God of love, he will deal with sins. Do not be deceived by the lies of the deceiver who says that God will never become angry and judge sin. He is a God of wrath. God's love will never erase his justice and holiness. You cannot approach him unless you deal with your sin. The good news, however, is that God has sent his Son, the great king prophesied in Micah, to break open the gate that holds us in bondage to sin. He alone can give us victory over the slavery of sin in our lives that keeps us under the judgment of God. Jesus alone can break down that gate and set us free.

For Consideration:

- Do you see evidence of false prophets in our society today? How can you recognize a false prophet?

- Why are people so easily deceived by false prophets?

- In what way has Satan been using to his advantage the doctrine of the love and compassion of God?

- Why is it so important to find a balance between the love and justice of God?

For Prayer:

- Thank the Lord that he is a God of justice who deals with sin.

- Do you know someone who is preaching the same message as the false prophets of Micah's day? Take a moment to pray that God would reveal himself to that person.

- Pray for those who are being deceived into believing the message of the false prophets. Ask God to open their hearts to the truth.

5

A Word to the Leaders

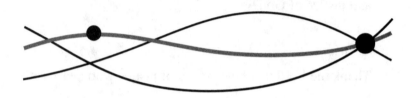

Read Micah 3:1–12

We saw in the last meditation that the false prophets of the land were misleading God's people. God judged the people because they delighted in the words of these false prophets. In this section, God proclaims his condemnation of these false prophets. He also has a word for the political leaders of the land.

Micah begins by speaking to the political rulers of Israel. As rulers, they should have guided God's people with justice. As leaders of God's people, they should have been seeking the well-being of the flock, but this was not the case. Listen to the accusation of God against these leaders.

Israel's rulers, according to Micah, did not follow principles of justice. The context indicates that they were only concerned about themselves. For them, justice amounted to doing whatever would lead to their own good. They cast aside all principles of godliness.

God's people were treated like animals. They were being

skinned, chopped up, broken into pieces, and put in a pan to be eaten. While this was not literally happening, the actions of Israel's leaders accomplished the same thing in principle. In order to enrich themselves, the rulers did not hesitate to treat those under them with cruelty. God's people were being sacrificed to satisfy the lusts of those in power.

God would hide his face from the leaders who did this. They would cry out to God, but he would not listen to them (verse 4). God was not blind to what they were doing to his people. These cruel rulers would be judged for the evil they had done. In their hour of need, they would cry out, but God would not help them.

Attention then shifts to the prophets. Micah accuses them of leading God's people astray. Notice how they worked. If someone paid them, they would prophesy peace. To those who did not pay, however, they pronounce doom and destruction (verse 5). Money and profit motivated their preaching. They preached whatever the people wanted to hear. They were not at all concerned about the Word of the Lord. Their only concern was their own personal gain.

The Lord's punishment of the prophets would be the same as the punishment of the secular leaders. God would hide his face from them. These prophets would no longer have any visions from the Lord (verse 6). No longer would they hear from God. Though they cried out to God, he would no longer answer them. They would hang their heads in shame because God would no longer answer their cries (verse 7).

In verses 8 and 9 Micah states that the Lord has filled him and called him to speak out against the leaders of the land who oppressed his people. Micah was aware of a special anointing from God to speak in power to the leaders of Israel and Judah. "I am filled with power, with the Spirit of the Lord, with justice and with might," says Micah. God's Spirit was on him. God called Micah to proclaim a very important message to his people.

Micah did not prophesy in his own strength and wisdom. We get the impression that Micah could not hold these words in. As Jeremiah the prophet said, God's words were like fire in his bones (Jeremiah 20:9). Not only did Micah know that the Lord was leading him to speak, he also knew the words that he was to speak. Listen to what God had to say through Micah to Israel's leaders of that day: Micah reminded them that they distorted justice and despised what was right. These men were evil. The Almighty God was angry with them. The words of Micah were hard. He did not hide the truth but spoke out against sin and evil.

Micah continued to tell the unjust rulers that they built their cities on bloodshed and wickedness. Their judges took bribes and their priests and prophets only served for money (verses 10–11). Israel's leaders served the god of materialism. They were not concerned about the people. They served for material gain.

The prophets and leaders of Micah's day were speaking what the people wanted to hear, but it was not the truth. Micah warned them that the day was coming when the judgment of God would fall on them. "Zion will be plowed like a field" (verse 12). He prophesied that the city would become a heap of rubble. Their glorious temple would be a mound of stone overgrown with thickets.

For the average person in the days of Micah, this would have been a very difficult word to swallow. They could never have imagined that such a thing could happen to their nation and temple. This, however, is exactly what happened.

Here we see the influence of materialism in Micah's day. Prophets and political leaders were serving for money, possessions, and respect. Their actions and decisions were clouded by their love of material things. We are called in this chapter to examine our own motives in serving the Lord.

The nation of Israel was judged because of the greed of her leaders and her people. May God set us free from the love of possessions and riches so that we can serve him as we should.

For Consideration:

- Are you a spiritual leader? Is it possible that you are serving God for your own glory?

- How does the life of Jesus and his self-sacrificing ministry compare with the ministry of the prophets and leaders of Micah's day?

- What kinds of things motivate us to take positions of leadership today? What should our real motives be?

For Prayer:

- Ask the Lord to reveal any way that you have been serving him for your own glory.

- Take a moment to pray for your political and spiritual leadership. Ask God to fill them with a desire for God alone.

- Ask God to set us free from the love of possessions.

6

Hope for Mount Zion

Read Micah 4:1–13

Micah has been prophesying that there will be difficult days ahead for the people of God. He reminds them, however, that the Lord will not forsake them forever. In his time, days of prosperity and blessing would return.

In chapter 3 Micah told his people that Jerusalem would be plowed under. The enemy would devastate their land. The judgment of God would fall because of the sins in the land. Micah reassured his people, however, that this judgment would not last forever. In the last days, the mountain of Zion would be restored. While Jerusalem would be plowed under, the mount of Zion would rise again to a place of honor. Just as a seed planted and plowed under the ground germinates and grows into a fruitful plant, so Israel would become a fruitful plant after she had been plowed under by the judgment of God.

God's intent in judging his people was to discipline them

so that they could become more useful in his hands. God works the same way in us. We need to understand this in our own walk with the Lord. Every one of us will go through periods of refining and purifying in our spiritual lives. In these times we ask the question, "Where are you, God?" What seems to be a harsh sentence is God's way of making us fruitful.

Micah prophesied that in the last days, the mountain of Zion would become the chief of all mountains. God would lift up his people and give them a place of honor. People would stream to the mountain of Zion. Notice in verse 2 that these people would be not only from the nation of Israel but from a variety of nations. These nations would come to the house of God as he brought these nations to himself. These foreigners would come to learn the ways of God and to follow his law. Notice that they would come of their own free will to the mount of Zion. Their hearts would be stirred and softened as they looked for the truth. They would come to meet the God of Abraham, Isaac, and Jacob. From Jerusalem the Word of the Lord would go out to the nations.

In part this prophecy was fulfilled in the days of the apostles, as recorded in the book of the Acts of the Apostles. In Acts we see how the Holy Spirit filled the apostles and used them to spread the good news of Christ to the far corners of the earth. While we can clearly see a partial fulfillment of this prophecy of Micah in the apostles and the spreading of the gospel in their day, what Micah tells us here seems to go beyond this.

Notice the extent of this wonderful promise to Israel. Not only would people from all nations turn to the Lord God of Israel, but through them the disputes of great nations would be settled. No longer would these nations prepare for war. Instead, their swords and weapons would be beaten into plowshares and pruning hooks. Instead of war and killing, they would focus their attention on peaceful activities. No longer would one nation take up war with another nation. They would live at peace with each other. Since the days of the apostles, however, we have seen one nation rise up against another. Nations are still building up arms to defend themselves. This indicates that the complete fulfillment of the prophecy of Micah has yet to take place.

Micah goes on to say that people would sit under their own vines and fig trees and no one would make them afraid (verse 4). The picture is one of prosperity and security. Notice that each person is sitting under "his *own* vine" and "his *own* fig tree." These people would not have to work for someone else. They would be cultivating their own land. There would be security and safety in the land because of the Lord's blessing.

Notice in verse 5 that these would also be times of real devotion to the Lord God. The people of Israel constantly wanted to be like the nations around them. As we examine the history of the people of God, they were always tempted to turn toward and serve the gods of the nations around them. Notice here, however, that something radically different would happen. Listen to what they were saying: "All the nations may walk in the name of their gods; we will walk in the name of the LORD our God for ever and ever" (verse 5). God would renew the hearts of his people. They would be devoted entirely to him and to him alone. They would want nothing to do with the gods of the nations. They would find in the God of Israel all they needed and desired. He would capture their hearts.

In those days God would bring the lame, the exiled, and the grieving to himself (verse 6). They would be strengthened, healed, and comforted as they sat under his reign. He would watch over them forever. His reign over them would not end. They would be cared for and become a very strong and powerful people. From their desolation they would be restored to prosperity and honor. God would extend his hand of compassion to those who had been sick and abandoned.

How and when did all this take place? Initially, the people of God returned from exile and rebuilt the city of Jerusalem under Ezra and Nehemiah. Though the Israelites were able to return to their land and rebuild their towns, God's people still suffered under the domination of foreign powers. Later, the Lord Jesus himself came and lived in their midst. He opened the door for forgiveness of sin and peace with God. Israel however, refused this salvation and chose rather to crucify her Messiah, rejecting his peace. In the days of the apostles, Israel became the center of missionary activity. From Israel the gospel went out to the ends of the earth. Spiritually, God's wonderful purpose for the world began to unfold in this part of the world. People from the nations came to the God of Israel and to the Messiah he sent to forgive sin. Each of these events has been a piece of the puzzle. Each piece has added to the fulfillment of the peace and prosperity of which Micah spoke. However, the pieces have not all come together to form the whole picture. The full realization of this prophecy has yet to be seen.

While Micah promised tremendous blessings to God's people, their immediate future was not so pleasant. They would come to these blessings through trial and sorrow (verse 9). They would cry out in pain like a woman in labor. This imagery is very powerful. While they would suffer, that suffering was a sign of greater things to come. Just as the pains of a woman in labor are a sign of imminent birth, so Israel's pains would be a sign of blessings to come. Scripture tells us that in the end times, believers should expect that things will become very difficult. Children will rise up against parents (see Matthew 10:21). Unbelievers will think they are doing God a favor by killing believers (see John 16:2). In the days of antichrist, those who refuse to bear his mark will be unable to buy or sell (Revelation 13:16–18). Before the blessing comes the pain of labor.

Have you suffered as a believer? There is hope for you. Before entering the Promised Land, the children of Israel spent forty years in the wilderness. Before leading God's people out of Egypt, Moses spent forty years in the desert. Before beginning his ministry, the Lord Jesus was tempted of the devil for forty days. For each of these cases, the blessing came after the labor pains. This is what Micah was telling his people in this passage. The blessing was coming, but for the moment, they would have to face the labor pains.

Verse 10 tells us that these pains would come for Israel, in part, in the form of exile into Babylon. God would send his people into captivity in Babylon, but he would not forsake them there. God would visit his people in the land of their exile. Are you facing a wilderness today? Be encouraged—God will not forsake you. He will redeem you from the hands of your enemies. This is a time of testing and preparation. This is a time of new growth and renewal. Let's not lose confidence in what God is doing. Let's bear patiently with him until he has finished the work he has begun in us. In his time we will give birth to his blessings.

There are times when we can feel overwhelmed. Micah said about his people: "Many nations are gathered against you" (verse 11). How many times in our wilderness experiences have we felt that everything that could possibly go wrong was going wrong? Micah said that this is how Israel would feel. There was one thing, however, that these enemies did not understand. They did not understand the thoughts of God and his plans for his people. Micah warned Israel's enemies that the day was coming when God's people would rise up and thresh their enemies (verse 13). God would restore his people to a place of honor and victory. He would give them horns of iron. The horn in Scripture is a symbol of authority and power. God would restore authority and power to his people. They would conquer in his name. He would also give them hoofs of bronze. With these hooves, they would trample their enemies like an ox treading the grain. Israel would break her enemies and consecrate their ill-gotten gains to the Lord who would give her victory.

Victory and blessing would come to Israel through trial and suffering. God's people needed to be prepared and refined for the battle that was ahead of them. God was refining his people. He was preparing them for great victory. Are you facing trial and suffering today? Don't lose heart. God has a purpose in your suffering. He will bring victory and blessing.

For Consideration:

- What trials are you facing today? What encouragement do you find in this passage?

- Why is it so hard for us to trust God in our trials? What keeps us from experiencing peace and joy in our pain?

- How often do great blessings come without suffering?

- How has God used trials and suffering in your life to equip you for greater blessing and ministry?

For Prayer:

- Thank the Lord that he does have a wonderful plan for your life.

- Ask him to help you to wait patiently on him in these trials.

- Ask him to forgive you for the times you have lost sight of him and his purposes in those trials.

- Take a moment to thank the Lord for the way he has used suffering and trials in your life to accomplish his greater glory.

7

Bethlehem's Blessing

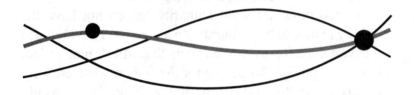

Read Micah 5:1–13

In the last meditation, Micah reminded the people of Jerusalem of the tremendous hope that was theirs in the days to come. Before seeing the fulfillment of that promise, however, they would have to pass through deep waters. Micah compared their hope to that of a woman in labor. Before she can know the joy of giving birth to a new child, she must pass through the pains of labor.

Micah speaks prophetically in this chapter. Though he speaks as if the events of this chapter have already taken place, they are future events. He begins in verse 1 by calling for the troops to be marshaled. The call was to prepare for battle. Jerusalem was under siege. The surrounding enemy had humbled Israel's leaders by striking them on the cheek with a rod. These things needed to happen before the tremendous blessing that was promised could be revealed. Before the victory came the humbling.

Very often, the Lord prepares us for victory by humbling

us. Some time ago, I was feeling my weakness and inability in the ministry to which God had called me. I remember praying at that time that the Lord would increase my authority in this ministry. The Lord showed me a picture of a pouch. As I looked at that pouch, the Lord seemed to say to me that this pouch was a pouch of humility. He then showed me that the authority I desired would be put inside that pouch. He made it clear to me that I could only have as much authority as my pouch of humility could contain. That picture has often been a real blessing to me.

All too often we want authority but do not have the humility to handle the authority we are given. The result can be devastating. Through the events that Micah prophesied, God would prepare his people for the authority and blessing he was going to give them in the future. God would accomplish this by stretching Israel's "pouch of humility."

After the days of trial, Micah prophesies that God would do a work among his people. That work would begin in one of the most insignificant of all their towns—Bethlehem. While this town was part of a small clan in the tribe of Judah, God would raise up a leader from Bethlehem for all his people. This would be no ordinary leader. This leader would be very special. Notice what Micah states about him in verse 2. His "origins are from of old, from ancient times." There is a footnote in the New International Version that says that another interpretation of the words "ancient times" is "eternity." In other words, the ruler who would be raised up from Bethlehem would be one who lived in eternity past. There is only one person whose origins are from eternity past. God alone is from eternity. Micah was telling his people that their Messiah would come from the insignificant and small town of Bethlehem.

I find it amazing that the Lord would choose the small and insignificant town of Bethlehem as Messiah's birthplace. Why did he choose to come to Bethlehem when there were other more significant places he could have chosen? Why did the Lord choose a very simple family to be born into as a man? Why did he choose to work with simple fishermen and not choose the elite spiritual leaders of the day? There is one thing for sure in all of this—God delights to use the simple and ordinary. What a blessing this is to us. How often I have taken courage from this thought. As I sit here and write this commentary, I am very conscious of the fact that God delights to use the simple. I am amazed to see how the Lord has taken these simple books and spread them around the world. If you are reading this book today, it is because God delights to bless the simple efforts of even the weakest of us. Maybe you look at yourself and your gifts and wonder how God could ever use you. God reveals himself to the poor and simple. Take courage in this.

For the moment, however, Israel would be abandoned. She would be in labor until the time for her delivery into a restored nation. At that future time, the rest of her brothers and sisters would come to join Israel (verse 3). What does Micah mean by this? From the time of her exile to the time when the Lord Jesus came to this earth, Israel was dominated by foreign powers. The Assyrians, Babylonians, Persians, Greeks, and Romans all dominated and controlled her. One day an angel appeared to Mary and told her that she would bring forth a son who would be called Jesus because he would deliver his people from their sins. Mary gave birth to our Lord and he ushered in a new age. Through his work as spiritual ruler of Israel, many nations came to know the God of Israel. The salvation that God promised extended to the far corners of the earth. In every corner of this earth today, there are people who are bowing the knee to the God of Abraham, Isaac, and Jacob. God's Spirit is moving in power over the surface of the earth. The spiritual strongholds of the enemy are being broken down.

Verse 4 reminds us that this great ruler (Jesus the

Messiah) would stand and be Israel's shepherd. The act of standing is a symbol of victory and authority. This Messiah would shepherd his sheep in the strength of the Lord and in the majesty of his name.

Micah tells us two important things about the reign of this Messiah. First, he would serve in the strength of God. He would have the authority and stamp of God's approval on his life and ministry. He would be anointed with the strength of God the Father for the ministry of shepherding his flock. We need not fear the enemy. Our shepherd is stronger than any foe that will come our way. We can place absolute confidence in him.

Second, Messiah's reign would be a reign of majesty. He would inspire awe and worship. He is worthy of our worship and praise because he reigns in the majesty of God himself. He is Lord and as such is deserving of our praise and worship.

Because Messiah reigns as our shepherd in the strength and majesty of the Lord God, we have no reason to fear. Micah tells us in verse 4 that God's people would live in security. Who can be against us as long as God is for us? (Romans 8:31). With Jesus as our Shepherd, we need not fear.

Micah told his people that this Messiah would be their peace. This peace would not only relate to security in the face of adversity but it would also refer to their relationship with God. Jesus brought peace between God and humanity. Jesus was the only one who could bring this peace.

Verse 4 reminds us that the greatness of this shepherd would reach the far corners of the earth. It is true that Jesus was the God of Israel, but his reign would extend to the whole earth. When Jesus died on the cross for our sins, he opened the door for people of all nationalities to come to know God. The apostles were sent to reach the world for the Lord Jesus. They moved in the power of the Holy Spirit, breaking down barriers and smashing strongholds. The kingdom of the Lord Jesus continues to expand even today as it has never expanded before. The greatness of the Lord Jesus is seen all over the earth, even as Micah prophesied.

There would be difficult times ahead for the people of God, but they could be sure of victory: "When the Assyrians invade and march against our land and fortresses, we will raise up seven shepherds and eight leaders" (verse 5). What did Micah mean? Could the reference to seven shepherds and eight leaders simply be a reference to the fact that when the enemy came, their leaders would be ready? These leaders would move Israel into victory over their foes. Verse 1 began with a call to marshal the troops. Does verse 5 go back to this thought? There is no particular need to find any significance in the numbers here. The general sense of the verse is quite clear. These leaders, whoever they might be, would lead Israel to victory. God's people would be ready for their enemy.

These leaders would crush Assyria when she came. They would conquer the land of Nimrod with the drawn sword. God would be the strength and deliverance of Israel. The reference to the land of Nimrod seems to be either a reference to the land of Babylon or Assyria. We see this in Genesis 10: "Cush was the father of Nimrod, who grew to be a mighty warrior on the earth. He was a mighty hunter before the LORD; that is why it is said, 'Like Nimrod, a mighty hunter before the LORD.' The first centers of his kingdom were *Babylon*, Erech, Akkad and Calneh, in Shinar. From that land he went to *Assyria*, where he built Nineveh, Rehoboth Ir, Calah and Resen, which is between Nineveh and Calah; that is the great city" (Genesis 10:8–12, emphasis added). From this we see that Nimrod was the founder of the great empires of Babylon and Assyria, which were enemies of the people of God in Micah's day.

Micah tells Israel to trust God in the day of trial. Israel

could face the foe with confidence in ultimate blessing. "When the Assyrian invades our land and marches through our fortresses, we will raise against him seven shepherds, even eight leaders of men," they said (verse 5). In other words, God's people would have final victory over their enemies. Who or what are your foes today? Can we say as did these people here that when the enemy comes, we will crush him because our God will deliver us? How many times have we run away with our tail between our legs because we did not have confidence in what God could do through us? Micah calls his people to absolute confidence in their God.

The conquering Assyrians and Babylonians would not keep God's people from accomplishing his wonderful purposes for them. Micah tells us in verse 7 that Israel would be "in the midst of many peoples like dew" and rain on the grass, which do not linger. God's people would be so numerous that they would be everywhere like the dew of the earth in the morning. Also like the dew, they would bring refreshment and renewal wherever they went. Although God would use conquering nations to discipline his sinful people, God would not allow these enemies to destroy his people. Despite the efforts of the enemy, God would bless his people, multiply them, and use them to bring the blessing he desired to the nations. We are the result of that blessing today.

Notice that Micah tells us that the dew does not linger for people. Is this not the case with the blessings of God? While they are as plentiful as the dew of the earth every morning, they do not wait for us. God offers us his blessings, but we must take them. The mercies of the Lord, like the dew of the earth, are new and fresh each morning. Like the manna that the children of Israel ate in the wilderness, each day brings its own supply of blessings from God. If the children of Israel did not take the manna offered to them that day, it disappeared. Either they took the blessing or it was taken from them. Praise him that there is a new supply tomorrow; but, how often we have missed the blessings meant for today. Israel would be scattered throughout the peoples of the earth for blessing and renewal like the dew. It would be up to those people to receive the blessings from God that came to them.

Notice also that Micah tells us in verse 8 that God's people would be among the nations like lions in the forest and among flocks of sheep. Not only would God's people be the bearers of blessing like the dew, but they would also be like hungry lions on the prowl. They would be sent to conquer and reclaim territory from the enemy. They would be victorious like hungry lions because God would deliver them. Their enemies would be defeated.

These two illustrations seem to contradict each other. In reality, however, they remind us of God's characteristics. He is a God of holiness. He is a roaring lion, a valiant warrior, and a mighty and all-powerful conqueror. He is also a God who refreshes like the dew. He is our Lord and he is our friend. These two attributes create a very healthy tension for us in our relationship with him. His fierceness and gentleness also show us that we too are to be both stern and tender as his servants. We impart blessing, but we are also warriors fighting for the glory of God. We are refreshing dew and prowling lions.

Micah reminded his people of the tremendous victory that would be theirs in God (verse 9). The day was coming when their hands would be lifted up in triumph over their enemies. God would destroy their enemies. Notice in verses 10–14 the extent of this victory. The Lord would destroy the enemies' horses and chariots. Their military strength would be no more. The God of Israel was bigger than any weapon an enemy could build against him. He is still bigger than any weapon that anyone can raise up against him today. While our weapons have become more complex, our God is bigger. Our horses have changed to fighting planes, bombs, and heavy artillery; but God is not threatened.

Micah announced that all enemy cities would be destroyed. The great evil strongholds would come down. What are the enemy's strongholds today? There are many strongholds in our day. Some of these relate to sins of lust, greed, and materialism. Some of these strongholds relate to political, educational, and economic institutions that have turned their backs on God's name. Some strongholds relate to spiritual areas where the enemy has been binding whole groups of people in darkness and oppression. One day God will break down all these strongholds.

Notice in verses 12–15 that witchcraft and worship of foreign gods would be purged from the nations. God is a jealous God who refuses to share his glory with another. He will take vengeance on those who have refused to live for him and seek his face.

There is a battle raging right now in our world. God is in the process of conquering the hearts and minds of a people to bring honor and glory to his name. He delights in taking simple and ordinary persons and accomplishing great things in them and through them. God offers blessing to all who will come to him. But be assured that those who turn from him will suffer his vengeance.

For Consideration:

- What encouragement is there for those of us who may feel insignificant in the work of the kingdom of God? (See verse 2.)

- Does your presence bring refreshment and blessing to those around you?

- Micah compares his people to the dew and the lion (gentle and yet stern). Have we found this balance in our churches today?

For Prayer:

- Thank the Lord that he can bring tremendous blessing through things small and insignificant.

- Ask the Lord to enable you to be like refreshing dew to those around you.

- Thank the Lord that he came to this world to offer us victory. Thank him that even though we may face deep struggle and trial, he is greater than anything the enemy can raise against us.

8

God's People on Trial

Read Micah 6:1–16

To understand what is happening in chapter 6 we need to see it as a court scene. Here God calls on the mountains and the hills to act as witnesses in the case he has against his people (verses 1–2).

God's case against his people really revolves around one central question: "My people, what have I done to you?" (verse 3). God speaks of how he had cared for his people throughout their history. He reminds them of how he had brought them up from the land of Egypt where they had been slaves for four hundred years (verse 4). He had heard their cry and rescued them from their enemies. He had placed Moses, Aaron, and Miriam over them as leaders. These leaders had cared for them and listened to all their grumbling and complaining for forty years in the wilderness where they wandered.

As God's people wandered through the wilderness, King Balak wanted to curse them. He hired Balaam to pronounce this curse, but God protected his people and would not permit Balaam to speak against them (verse 5). God challenged his people to consider the things that had happened to them from Shittim to Gilgal. The children of Israel had been in Shittim when Balak hired Balaam to curse them (see Numbers 25:1). Gilgal, according to Joshua 4:19, was where the children of Israel had crossed the Jordan River into the Promised Land.

God challenged his people to consider how he had protected and provided for them throughout their history. Never once had he failed them. As they considered these things, Micah challenged them to ask themselves what God had ever done to them that they should treat him as they were treating him that day.

There is something here for us as well. What God is challenging his people to do is to examine all his kindness and mercy toward them. How important it is for us to do the same. Consider for a moment all that God has done for you. Consider how he has protected and provided for you. Consider all his blessings in your life and ask yourself if your relationship with him reflects the gratitude you owe him.

In light of God's tremendous patience and compassion toward his people, Micah challenges them to consider what God required of them in return (verse 6). Was God happy with all their sacrifices of burnt offerings? Did they really think that thousands of rams and ten thousand rivers of oil would please him? If they sacrificed their own firstborn for their sins, would this really have delighted his heart? Was God only looking for sacrifices and offerings? Would the blood of a goat be enough to pay the Lord for his faithfulness to them?

Today we no longer sacrifice rams and bulls. The questions, however, remain: Is God looking for our money and possessions? Is it enough that we give a tithe of all we earn? Is God content when we show up in church on Sunday and go to the mid-week meeting? Is this all that God wants?

Micah assures Israel that God is not bloodthirsty, delighting in seeing blood and animal sacrifice. God is looking for three things from his people. First, God wanted a people who act justly (verse 8). From the context this justice is to be demonstrated in community relationships. In verses 9–12 the Lord speaks to his people about their ill-gotten treasures, their dishonest scales, and their bags of false weights.

Notice how Micah mentions particularly here the "short ephah." The ephah was a dry measurement. The grain was measured in ephahs. The reference here to a short ephah shows us what was happening in the land at that time. When a seller measured a short ephah, the buyer was receiving less than the expected quantity. Micah challenges his people regarding such lies and dishonesty. He reminds them that more than their sacrifices and offerings, more than their faithful attendance at the yearly festivals and celebrations, God is interested in their relationships with each other. God noticed that his people were cheating and disrespecting each other, and he would hold them accountable.

God's heart has not changed over the years. Scripture is very clear on this matter. God challenged his people in the New Testament to leave their gifts at the altar and be reconciled with their brothers and sisters before they offered their gifts (Matthew 5:23). Jesus told his people that, if they wanted to be forgiven, they would first need to forgive others (Matthew 6:14–15). We cannot separate our relationships from our worship of God. Psalm 133 tells us that God pours out his blessing on those who dwell in unity. God is more interested in just and right relationships between brothers and sisters than he is in all our sacrifices. God's people were coming to him with their sacrifices, but

God was not interested in those sacrifices because of the broken relationships in their communities.

Second, Micah tells Israel that God requires mercy (verse 8). Mercy is favor and kindness shown to those who are undeserving. God reminded his people of how he had treated them in the wilderness. They had not served him but had grumbled and complained all the way. They did not deserve his compassion and kindness, but God poured it on them anyway. They were not perfect, but God accepted them.

Remember that the Lord chose to work with Judas even though he knew from the beginning that Judas would betray him. Jesus still worked with him. One day when Jesus was in the temple, some men brought an adulterous woman to him. The religious leaders wanted to stone her, but Jesus showed compassion and mercy to her. He chose to forgive and offer her a second chance. Where would any of us be today without the mercy and compassion of God?

We have seen believers separate and argue over small and insignificant issues. We have seen believers lift up their doctrine and practice to such a level that they reject anyone who does not believe or practice faith exactly as they do. As humans, we do not forget sin easily. Like the Pharisees of Jesus' day, we sometimes practice the letter of the law but neglect to show mercy toward each other. Jesus walked with sinners; we have a tendency to reject them. Jesus forgave sin; we have a tendency to remember it.

Micah tells us here that God desires mercy. He desires that we treat each other as he has treated us. Mercy is given to those who do not deserve favor. We can come faithfully to church and give our sacrificial gifts, but if we do not demonstrate mercy, we fall short of God's standard. Micah tells us that, more than all our sacrifices, God is seeking a people who will demonstrate mercy toward each other.

Third, Micah states that God requires his people to walk

humbly before him (verse 8). To walk humbly before God we must be in submission and obedience to his will and purposes. To walk humbly before God we must be willing to put him first in all matters. We must be willing to listen to him when he speaks to us. When the Holy Spirit brings conviction of sin, we must repent and surrender to him. When the Lord uses someone else to challenge our sin, we must submit to their counsel. Are we willing to recognize the error of our ways? To walk humbly with God is to recognize him as Lord and willingly bow the knee in obedience to him.

In verses 9–12 God shows his people how they had fallen short of this standard. They had been dishonest in their dealings with each other (verse 10). They had been oppressing and lying to each other (verse 12). These things stood as a barrier between them and the blessing of God.

In verses 13–16 God shows his people that his wrath has already fallen on them. They were already being destroyed because of their sins. They had food to eat, but they would never be satisfied. The sword would take what they had stored up and saved. They planted but they would not harvest any fruit. They pressed olives and crushed grapes, but they would not be able to enjoy the fruit of their labors. God removed his blessing because Israel had not acted justly, shown mercy, or walked humbly before him.

God's people walked after the statutes of Omri and followed the practices of Ahab (verse 16). Both of these kings were known for their evil ways (1 Kings 16:25, 30). Because God's people had followed these wicked examples, they would be given over to ruin. They would become the scorn of the nations around them.

The same thing is true for us today. Jesus tells us that the world will know that we are Christians by our love for each other (John 13:35). The unbelieving world will be tempted to mock the name of Jesus when they see believers who do not treat each other with justice and mercy. We cannot afford to downplay the importance of developing deep relationships in the body of Christ.

One day the Lord Jesus was asked what he considered to be the greatest commandment. He responded: "'Love the Lord your God with all your heart and with all your soul and all your mind.' This is the first and greatest commandment. And the second is like it: 'Love your neighbor as yourself'" (Matthew 22:37–39).

This is exactly what Micah is telling us here. In light of all that God has done for us, we need to be a people who love the Lord our God by walking humbly with him and who love our neighbors as ourselves by showing justice and mercy in all our dealings.

For Consideration:

- Consider for a moment the tremendous blessings you have received from the hand of the Lord. What are some of those blessings?

- Take a moment to examine your own life in light of the threefold requirement of God as described by Micah. Are you living your life in the light of these requirements? Where do you fall short?

- Why are relationships in the body of Christ so important?

- Why is it so easy for us to fall into the trap of measuring spirituality by how many times a person attends church or by how much he gives to the Lord?

For Prayer:

- Ask the Lord to help you to live according to the standard that he lays out in Micah 6.

- Are there people in the body of Christ whom you have trouble loving? Ask the Lord to help you to love them as he loves them.

- Ask the Lord to show you if there are any areas in your life where you are not walking humbly before God.

- Thank the Lord for the wonderful mercy and compassion he has shown you.

9

Who Is Like Our God?

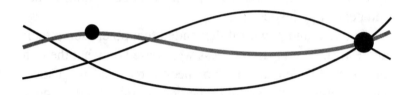

Read Micah 7:1–20

C hapter 7 begins with a scene of misery and despair. Micah describes what is going to happen to God's people. To do this he uses a picture of a gardener.

The gardener comes to harvest the fruit of the summer. He arrives at his vineyard to gather the fruit but finds that the vines are empty. This picture is very similar to the picture the Lord Jesus gave us of the parable of the man who left his land in the hands of his servants and went away on a long trip (Matthew 25:14). When he returned, he expected to see fruit. If the Lord were to return today to reclaim the fruit that he has planted in your life, what would he find? Israel had no fruit to show the heavenly gardener.

Verses 2–6 describe what the Lord, as a gardener, found in Israel. The godly had been swept from the earth (verse 2). As the Lord looked around the land, he could not find any individuals who were committed to serving him with their whole heart (verse 2). Instead, he only found people who were quick to shed blood. They hunted each other as those who seek their prey with a net. The land was full of evil. All the people were violent and unjust in their dealings with each other.

Micah records in verse 3 that both hands were skilled in doing evil. That is to say, the people of God were so good at doing evil they could do it with both hands! The rulers demanded gifts. They used their positions to get rich by abusing those they should have been serving. The legal system of the land was corrupt, with judges taking bribes and perverting justice.

The rich and powerful demanded that others serve their interests. Decisions in business were based on what the rich and powerful demanded. Poor people received no justice. Their interests were ignored. The rich got richer and the poor got poorer.

Micah laments that the best people of Israel were like briers, and the most upright were like thorn hedges. If you have ever had to deal with briers and thorn hedges, you can understand what Micah is saying here. If you walk among briers and thorn hedges, you will very soon be scratched and cut. This is what the best of the people were like. They used their words and deeds to cut and scratch everyone they met.

In verse 4 Micah reminds his people that God saw what was happening in the land. The day of their punishment had come. They would now have to account for their actions.

Micah observes in verse 5 that things had become so bad that no one in the land was trustworthy. Micah warns the people not to trust their neighbors, their closest friends, or even their spouses. The society in Israel had degenerated to the point where everyone was concerned only for personal gain and self-interest. No one could trust anyone else to be honest in a transaction or a relationship. Everything people said or did would be used against them to further someone else's selfish cause.

Relationships did not stand in the way of the people furthering their own ends. If by betraying a friend or spouse, individuals could advance their own causes, they would do so in an instant. In our age where marriage vows are as easily broken as they are made, are we not equally as guilty of this crime? What would God say to our society that willingly kills by abortion children who are considered an inconvenience or stand in the way of the parents' goals and agendas?

Micah addressed his prophecy to a people who lacked common decency and human respect. God's people were not showing mercy and justice. They were not walking humbly before their God. A son would dishonor his father, and a daughter would rise up against her mother. A daughter-in-law would stand up against her mother-in-law. Family relations meant nothing. The family unit was breaking down. You can be sure that if there was no respect at the level of the family, then there would certainly be no respect on other levels of society either. There was a devastating breakdown of social relationships. A person could count on no one, not even family members. As God looked down on the nation of Israel, he saw moral chaos and disorder.

What hope was there for a society that had gone this far? Micah records in verse 7 that he watched for the Lord in hope and knew that the God of his salvation had heard his prayers. Micah did not give up hope. He knew that the situation in his land was desperate. To all appearances the situation was beyond repair, but there was still a God in heaven. No matter how bad the situation had become, Micah reminds us that there was still reason to hope in the Lord.

In verse 8 Micah tells Israel's enemies not to gloat. Although God's people had fallen, they would rise again. Yes, they were sitting in the dark, but the Lord would come and be their light. Yes, they had sinned and would feel the wrath of God, but the day would come when he would give them victory (verse 9). They would again see God's righteousness demonstrated. The Lord God was bigger than their sin and rebellion.

Micah prophesied that the day was coming when God's enemies would be covered with shame (verse 10). These enemies mocked Israel by asking where her God was. There was no visible evidence of God in the land. These enemies would see the downfall of Israel and wonder if she had been abandoned by her God. The day was coming, however, when those who mocked God and his people would see a clear demonstration of his power and glory. In that day God would defeat Israel's enemies and trample them under foot.

As we look at the powerful forces of darkness that are at work in our land today, we wonder how it could ever be that they would be destroyed. How can righteousness triumph when darkness and evil are so powerful in our land? Micah tells us that we have every reason to hope in the Lord. God will defeat the forces of evil. We will see them trampled under our feet. The Lord God made this promise to Adam and Eve in the Garden of Eden. He told them that the day was coming when the Lord himself would trample on the head of the serpent and bring victory to his people (Genesis 3:15). Micah confirms this in this passage.

The day of building walls and expanding boundaries was coming again for God's people. God had not forsaken them (verse 11). The day was coming when Assyria and Egypt, the principle enemies of the people of God, would bow the knee to Israel in honor and respect. From sea to sea and from mountain to mountain, people would come to bless Israel. Earlier, Micah prophesied that many nations would come to the mountain of Jerusalem to seek Israel's God and to learn his ways (4:2). Even those who mocked God would one day realize the power of his name and bow their knees before him.

In verse 13 Micah predicts that the earth will become desolate because of its evil inhabitants. Micah asks God, however, to pasture his people (verse 14). Micah reminds Israel that God will come to his people in their time of trouble. They will graze in rich pasturelands of Bashan and Gilead. Both these locations were known for their rich and luscious pastures (Ezekiel 39:18; Song of Solomon 6:5). Though their society was broken and destroyed, God's people would again dwell in rich and pleasant pastures blessed by God. God promised to show them the signs and wonders he had previously demonstrated to their ancestors in Egypt. Their enemies would no longer ask them where their God was. He would be evident in their midst.

The nations around Israel would be ashamed (verse 16). They would be ashamed not only of how they had treated God's people but also of their own powerlessness before the God of Israel. Micah foresaw that these nations would lay their hands to their mouths in astonishment and wonder. Their ears would become deaf, as if they could not take in what they were hearing. It is hard to imagine the powerful leaders of our day standing back in awe as they look on in wonder at the power of God. The history of the church, however, has shown us many times that even the hardest of individuals can be broken by the Lord God and the power of his Holy Spirit.

These nations, writes Micah, will lick the dust like a snake, so great will be their humiliation (verse 17). They will come trembling out of their dens like fierce lions turned into meek kittens. They will come to the Lord God of Israel. They will recognize their sin and tremble before the one true God. How we long to see such a powerful demonstration of God and his wonderful power moving in us and through us to the nations in our day. Micah promises that this day will come.

In verses 18–20 Micah concludes by pointing again to God. Was there ever a God who forgave sin as did Israel's God? This great God took a ruined people who had no longer even any respect for each other, forgave them, and then used them to demonstrate his power to the nations.

Israel's God, rejoices Micah, does not stay angry forever (verse 18). He delights to show mercy. This does not mean that he will not get angry. His anger is real. He does not stay angry, however. He extends his hands to people who do not deserve his kindness and compassion. He loves to show benevolence and care to those who do not deserve it.

The Lord God treads our sins under foot and hurls them into the depths of the sea. They will never be seen again. They will never be remembered again. He will remember his promises to Abraham and to Jacob. He will not forget his people.

What a wonderful promise we have here in this passage. I do not know where you are today. I do not know the condition of your church or your town. What I do know, however, is that God is a wonderful and compassionate God who can take the worst situation and make something wonderful out of it. He can take the most rebellious sinners and demonstrate his compassion and love through them. Don't lose hope. God is a God of the impossible, and Micah promises tremendous things for those who wait on him.

For Consideration:

- Compare the situation at the beginning of this chapter with your society. What similarities do you see?

- What enemies does the Lord need to overcome in your life or in the life of your church? What comfort do you take from this chapter today?

- What kind of person is the Lord God able to use, according to Micah in this passage?

For Prayer:

- Thank the Lord for the tremendous hope Micah gives us here in this passage.

- Ask God to demonstrate his power in your own society and church, as he promised through Micah.

- Ask God to forgive you for doubting his ability to transform your society, church, or personal life.

Nahum

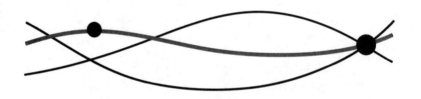

10

Nineveh's Fall

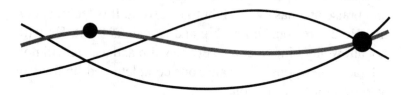

Read Nahum 1:1–15

The book of Nahum is a prophecy against the city of Nineveh, the capital of the Assyrian empire. For a long time the Assyrians had oppressed the citizens of Israel and Judah. We are not told here when Nahum prophesied, but it was obviously during a period when Assyria was strong and powerful. The prophecy of Nahum predicted the fall of Assyria because of her oppression of God's people.

Verse 1 tells us that this is the prophecy of "Nahum the Elkoshite." We know nothing about Nahum apart from this book. Scholars are not sure about the exact location of the city of Elkosh. Nahum's name means "comfort" or "reassurance." The apostle Paul tells us in 1 Corinthians 14:3 that the person who speaks prophecy speaks comfort, strength, and encouragement. This is what Nahum did. His words of comfort were not to Nineveh but to the children of

God under Assyrian oppression. God's people were in need of reassurance and comfort at this time in their history.

Nahum begins his prophecy by reminding Israel of the great jealousy and wrath of God (verse 2). Jealousy is usually considered a negative characteristic. Often, we confuse jealousy with covetousness or lust. To covet or to lust is to desire what does not belong to us or what we have no right to possess. There is, however, a jealousy that is legitimate. The jealousy spoken of here is a jealousy that God has for his people and his glory. He desires our worship and praise and has every right to receive it. It is legitimately his. He desires our fellowship and is jealous for it. He will not allow anything to come between him and us. He will not tolerate other gods. He wants our complete and undivided attention for himself alone.

God was angry because of what the enemy was doing to his children. Nineveh had oppressed his children and made their lives difficult. God would not stand idly by and watch this injustice. He would take vengeance on his enemies for the sake of his children.

Nahum announces that God maintains his anger against his foes (verse 2). Nahum goes on to explain in more detail what he means. Although God is very slow to anger, very patient, and shows great forgiveness and compassion even to the worst sinner, he is a God of great power and holy justice and will punish sin. We are living in a time when preaching on the wrath of God is slowly declining. Some have chosen to preach that God is only a God of love and forgiveness. God is indeed a God of forgiveness, love, and compassion. Nahum, however, reminds us that God's wrath is also very real. We see it in the storms and the whirlwinds of nature.

Living on the islands of Mauritius and Reunion in the Indian Ocean, we saw first-hand the power of the wind in the cyclones that passed from time to time through that region of the world. At times these winds were terrifying. To avoid them, we locked ourselves in our home and closed all the shutters. These winds and storms were simple reminders of the reality of the power and wrath of Almighty God.

Nahum tells his people that clouds in the sky are the stirring up of God's feet. As the Israelites walked on their dirt roads, they stirred up dust under their feet. Nahum uses this image to remind his people of the vastness of God by telling them that the clouds of the sky are the dust under God's feet.

When this awesome God rebukes the sea, it dries up. The Israelites knew this to be true in their own history. They had crossed the Red Sea on dry land. If you have ever stood by the shore of the ocean and watched the waves crashing on the coast, you can understand the power of the sea. The sound of the voice of God can dry up these great seas (verse 4). God speaks and the rivers run dry. Bashan and Carmel wither, and Lebanon's blossoms fade when the Lord speaks. Bashan and Carmel were known for their rich pasturelands. Lebanon was known for its great forests of tall cedars. God could take away all these blessings with a single word from his lips.

The mountains quake at the presence of the Lord. This was what happened in the days of Moses when the Lord descended on Mount Sinai. In the Lord's presence, the hills and the earth melt and shake. All the inhabitants of the earth tremble when he reveals his presence.

Who among us can withstand such a God? When he becomes angry, who can endure it? His wrath is poured out like fire (verse 6). It destroys whatever is in its path. The rocks of the earth are shattered before him.

We are helpless before such wrath and anger. It is a dreadful thing to stir up God's anger. The eternal flames of hell testify to this fierce and holy justice. The Bible tells us that in the day the Lord returns, people will hide themselves in caves and in the mountains, calling on the rocks to fall on them to hide them from the fierce anger of this Holy Lord (Luke 23:30). We must never forget his anger. A deeper understanding of his anger can show us how real his compassion and forgiveness is. Only when we understand what he has rescued us from can we truly appreciate his grace and mercy.

So that he does not paint a one-sided picture, Nahum announces that the Lord is also very good (verse 7). He is a refuge in time of trouble. He cares for those who trust in him. In him and under his grace and mercy, we are protected and secure. Nothing can harm us. How wonderful it is to have the assurance that we are sheltered and protected.

While the Lord's goodness and protection are very real for those who trust in him, his wrath comes like a flood and consumes his enemies. When the waters of God's wrath come crashing down on the Assyrians, they would not be able to resist. Nineveh would be pursued to the darkness. Darkness represents hopelessness and death. Nineveh would be consumed and destroyed.

Nineveh's plans against God and his people would be foiled (verse 9). So complete would be her devastation that trouble would not come a second time to her. In other words, God would destroy her with one swipe of his hand. He would not need to take a second swipe. Nineveh would be entangled with thorns. Trouble would come on her and she would not be able to escape.

Verse 10 tells us that Israel's enemy would become drunk from her own wine. Nineveh had poured out her oppression on the people of God; now she would taste her own medicine. She would drink deeply from the wine of God's fury. Even as she had done to Israel, so it would be done to her. Like dry stubble, the fire of God's wrath and anger would consume her.

Nahum prophesies in verse 11 that among the people of Nineveh is one who plots evil against the Lord. This could possibly refer to her leaders who had been oppressing the people of God. Nahum predicted that Nineveh's numerous allies would be cut off. No one would help her in the day of God's anger. Her doom was sure. How important this is for us to understand. The unsaved will have no one to hide behind in the day of God's wrath. No one will be able to help them when God passes his final sentence of judgment.

Nahum turns his attention for a moment to the people of God. "Although I have afflicted you, O Judah," says God, "I will afflict you no more" (verse 12). God allowed his people to be afflicted by the Assyrians for a time as a means of refining judgment. He used that affliction in their lives to do a wonderful work of grace. God is able to use even the evil our enemies do to us to accomplish great good in our lives. This does not excuse our enemies for what they have done; but it is comforting to know that God can use even their insults and oppression to draw us closer to himself.

What is important for us to see here is that God promised his people an end to their affliction. The yoke of their oppression would be broken. He would tear away their shackles. They would be given new hope and life. In God they would overcome. What a wonderful promise. As we said in the beginning of this meditation, "Nahum" means "comfort" or "reassurance." It is easy to see here how this vision from Nahum would bring that comfort to God's people.

As for Nineveh, she would have no more descendants (verse 14). Assyria would perish as a nation. Her images and idols would be destroyed. She would be no more.

God's people were called to rejoice (verse 15). The prophecy would not delay. Already, proclaimed Nahum, you could hear the feet of those bringing good news coming over the mountains. Messengers came to bear the news that God had set his people free. Announcements of deliverance and peace were on their way to God's oppressed people.

This news of peace was cause for celebration. God's people were called to celebrate their festivals and fulfill their vows to the Lord. Their enemies were defeated. They would no longer be overcome. They were completely and totally free to worship the Lord.

This same message of peace comes to us today through the Lord Jesus. From the mountain of Calvary, he announced that his people no longer had to be bound under the domination of the enemy of sin. Jesus came to offer us complete freedom. He tells us that we can have peace with God through his sacrifice. We no longer have to be under the wrath of God.

For Consideration:

• Why do you suppose we hear so little preaching in our day on the wrath of God?

• How does a proper understanding of the wrath of God help us to appreciate his grace and mercy?

• From what do you need to be freed? What encouragement do you receive from this chapter?

For Prayer:

• Thank the Lord that through the Lord Jesus you have been set free from the anger and wrath of God.

• Thank him that he comes to give you total victory over the enemy's oppression.

• Are there particular areas in your life where you still struggle with sin? Ask God to give you complete victory.

11

God's Clash
with Nineveh

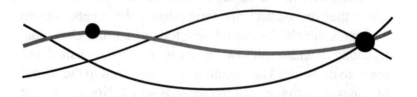

Read Nahum 2:1–13

Chapter 2 of Nahum is filled with graphic detail and imagery. Nahum prophetically describes a great battle scene. Nineveh was about to fall.

Nahum announced that the attackers were advancing against the city of Nineveh. The city was called on to prepare for a great battle. "Guard the fortress, watch the road, brace yourselves, marshal all your strength!" (verse 1). Nineveh's enemy was advancing on her.

Verse 2 tells us the reason for this attack against Nineveh. God wanted to restore the splendor of Jacob in order to reveal his power and his glory to the world. For a long time, Nineveh had laid his people waste and ruined their vines. God was again going to do a mighty work through his people. They would once more be a strong and glorious people.

How we need, as believers, to see this happen in our day. For long enough, the people of God have been unfruitful and weak. For long enough, the enemy has trampled our churches. Now is the time for the people of God to be strengthened for battle. Now is the time for us to be the instruments of God's glory and light in a dark and decaying world.

Nahum prophesied that a great army would invade Nineveh (verse 3). These soldiers would carry red shields. They would be dressed in scarlet uniforms. Red is the color of blood. Would this army's clothes be stained scarlet by the blood of those they had slain?

The metal of the invader's chariots would flash in the sun as they rushed back and forth through the streets. Nahum compares the chariots to flaming torches darting about like lightning. Nahum foresaw the spears being brandished and ready to do battle. The invading army was seen in the streets of Nineveh, moving with tremendous speed. Nothing would stop the destruction of Nineveh.

As this fearful army moved about the city, Nineveh was called to defend herself. Her leader summoned the elite of the army to rush to the wall and defend against the charging enemy. Nineveh was depicted as so panicked by this attack that as her troops rushed to the wall, they stumbled on the way. The army of Nineveh was no match for its enemy.

Nahum prophesied that the river gate would be thrown open.[1] Like a mighty flood, the enemy would crash through the gate into the city of Nineveh. The palace, a symbol of her government and power, would collapse. Nahum decreed that the city would be carried away into exile, just as she had done to God's people.

Nahum describes this exile quite vividly in verses 7 and 8. He compares the city to a great pool of water that is quickly draining. The river gate had been broken through and the result was a massive exodus of her people, like water pouring out of a large pool. As the inhabitants left, the slave girls moaned and beat their breasts in grief. Nahum predicted the cry of those who were more stubborn, calling out to the fleeing exiles: "Stop! Stop!" But no one listened to this cry. They continued to leave the city. No one wanted to return. Nineveh was quickly emptied of her inhabitants.

As the inhabitants left, the great army of God would plunder the city, stripping it of its gold and silver. Nineveh's vast treasures would be handed over to her enemies. The nation that was once great and powerful would stand naked and helpless before the Lord and his mighty army.

The hearts of the inhabitants of Nineveh would melt. They would lose hope. There would be nothing but despair. Knees would give way. Bodies would tremble. Faces would show pain, fear, and anguish. This would indeed be a terrible day. Nineveh's end would come. Never would they have thought that this would happen to them. Nineveh was powerful and inspired fear wherever she went. But soon she would be crushed and broken.

In verses 11–13 Nahum compares Assyria to a lion. The lion represents power and fierceness. As a nation, Assyria was like a lion ripping and tearing apart their prey. The situation, however, would change. "Where now is the lions' den?" asks Nahum. This lion would no longer have a home. Nineveh, the great lion, would become homeless.

There in the lions' den, the great lion used to feed her cubs. These cubs had nothing to fear. The lion would go out into the fields and forests to find food for each cub. She would bring back her spoils and feed her family. She filled her den with the spoils of her many conquests. Nineveh was the lions' den. Her military and political leaders were the lions who went out among the nations, killing and ravaging. When they had returned from their hunts, they enriched and fed their families with the spoils of war. The city of Nineveh, like the lions' den, was filled with trophies of many conquests. Soon, however, her ill-gotten riches would be given to another.

God had seen the evil deeds of the Assyrians and would

punish them. God would burn the chariots they had used to attack the nations. The sword would devour their young. Their own families would perish by the sword of the Lord's judgment. All they had taken from others would be stripped from them. The voices of their messengers would no longer be heard in the land. They would be no more.

God was going to judge sin. Nineveh had lived with a false hope that her military strength was sufficient. She would be destroyed. Similarly, there are many things we can depend on today. Outside of Christ, however, there is no hope. We dare not place our confidence in anything other than the Lord our God. He alone is worthy of our confidence. In him alone can we be secure.

For Consideration:

- Nineveh depended on her army and her military strength. What kind of things do we depend on today?

- We have a picture of the triumph of God over his enemies here in this chapter. Does this describe the church of our day? What are the enemies of the church in our day?

- Is your life a life of victory? What do you need to conquer in your life today?

- What encouragement do you find in the fact that the Lord will overcome the enemies of his people? What enemies has he already overcome in your life?

For Prayer:

- Thank the Lord that he will show the world his incredible majesty and glory.

- Do you have loved ones who have not understood the danger of being outside of Christ? Take a moment to pray that the Lord would open their eyes to the reality of the danger they are facing. Ask the Lord to bring them to himself.

- Ask the Lord to show you the victories you need to experience in your own life.

- Ask the Lord to make your church a victorious church.

- Thank the Lord that he is an overcoming God.

12

The End of Nineveh

Nahum 3:1–19

The prophet Nahum had a way with words. His language is poetic. The reader can hear and see the details as he describes them in this passage.

Nineveh's end would come. "Woe to the city of blood," wrote Nahum (verse 1). As the principle city of Assyria, Nineveh represented the entire nation. She was a bloody city. The Assyrians were a cruel people. They were responsible for the loss of many lives through their wars and battles.

Notice also that the city of Nineveh was full of lies (verse 1). Honesty no longer mattered. Nineveh was filled with the plunder of the nations around them. Her citizens had become rich from taking what belonged to others. They stole, cheated, and killed to obtain their wealth. The city was never without victims (verse 1). There did not seem to be any time when someone was not being killed, cheated, or robbed to satisfy the lusts of the nation's leaders.

Verses 2 and 3 describe for us a scene of war. The battle

that rages is the battle that God is raging against Nineveh. As we listen, we hear the sound of cracking whips in the distance. Chariot riders beat their horses as they rush to and from the battle scene. We hear the clatter of chariot wheels as they rush over the ground. Horses are galloping. Chariots are jolting. There is rush and excitement all around.

The invading cavalry is charging into the city of Nineveh. Swords are flashing in the sun as the invaders swing at the inhabitants of the great city. Spears glitter too in this great battle. There are many casualties. Bodies pile up without number (verse 3). People stumble over these bodies strewn on the ground.

The scene before us is one of terrible destruction and chaos. The army of Nineveh had been slaughtered. They had no hope against this powerful army of God's judgment. The Assyrian army, which had caused such terror on the earth, now had fallen prey to terror.

Verse 4 tells us that all this happened because of wanton lust. As a people, the god of lust had trapped the Assyrians. Lust, like a great prostitute, had lured them into her trap. This great mistress entrapped them by her witchcraft. The moment they gave in to her, she closed her trap around them. She blinded them and controlled their every move and decision.

Lust is a very powerful enemy. Lust will blind our eyes to the things we already have. Lust is short-sighted and does not count the cost. It is blind to the consequences of its actions. Lust controls, dominates, and manipulates. It has no respect for people or things. It cares nothing for the laws of God. It will sacrifice everything to have the object of its attention. Lust led Assyria to kill, steal, and cheat. Ultimately, it was the reason for her judgment and destruction.

Still today the victims of lust can be seen everywhere. Some, through lust for pleasure, have broken up their homes and families. Some, out of a lust for power, have resorted to killing and dishonesty to obtain that power. Others, out of a lust for money and possessions, have tossed aside family and friends in their endless pursuit of the object of their unhealthy desire. Lust will very quickly turn us from God and his Word. It is the source of many evils.

"I am against you," announced God to the city of Nineveh (verse 5). "I will lift your skirts over your face." God would show the nations who Nineveh really was. He would expose the hidden things in her life—her shameful ways. God's anger against the city of Nineveh was very real. "I will pelt you with filth," he decreed (verse 6). God would make a spectacle out of Nineveh. People would see her shame and watch her fall. The Lord would treat her with the contempt she deserved.

All those who would see Nineveh in her hour of need would flee from her (verse 7). When Nineveh lay in ruins, no one would mourn for her. No one would be found to comfort her—everyone would turn away. No one would care that she was destroyed. No one would miss her. She had hurt too many people and made too many enemies. She would be alone in her hour of need.

"Are you better than Thebes?" asked God (verse 8). The great city of Thebes had been situated on the Nile River. She had enjoyed the prosperity that the Nile brought. Water surrounded her and she had flourished. The water not only brought her wealth and prosperity but was also her protection. Any army approaching her first had to cross the river. This had been a very definite advantage to Thebes.

Thebes also had gained many allies. Nahum mentions Cush (Ethiopia), Egypt, Put, and Libya. In a time of war, these nations had come to the aid of Thebes. She had seemed to be invincible. Who could overcome this powerful city with her defenses and allies?

God reminded Nineveh, however, that Thebes, the great city, had been taken captive and sent into exile. Her children were dashed to pieces by the attacking forces (verse 10). Lots were cast for her nobles and her greatest men were put in chains. If such a thing could happen to the city of Thebes, could it not also happen to the city of Nineveh?

In verse 11 Nahum reminds Nineveh that she will become drunk. She would drink deeply from the cup of God's wrath. As a nation, she would go into hiding in an attempt to flee from the wrath of God. Like Thebes, however, Nineveh would also be destroyed.

Nahum compares Nineveh's fortresses to a fig tree in verse 12. The fig tree was shaken and its fruit had fallen to the ground. The enemy was at the foot of the tree shaking it so that the ripe figs would fall to the ground and end up in the mouth of the enemy. Nineveh would be shaken like that fig tree. The enemy would eat the fruit of her prosperity.

Nahum comments, "Look at your troops—they are all women!" (verse 13). The cultural understanding here is that Nineveh's troops were weak and helpless. They could do nothing about the approaching army. Remember that the Assyrian army was at one time the most powerful army on the earth. God, however, had taken her strength from her. How dependent we are on God for our strength and ability. Sometimes we believe that we are invincible. Somehow, we believe that we will always have our health and strength. Nahum shows us that God is able to take strength from even the most powerful army on the surface of the earth. We should never take for granted what God has given us.

The gates of the city of Nineveh would be wide open to the enemy (verse 13). The bars that kept these gates shut would be burned off so the enemy could storm into the city. Nahum taunted the people to quickly draw water to mix clay and mortar to strengthen and repair their defenses (verse 14). The Assyrians would make a futile effort to keep the enemy out. They would not succeed. The fire would devour them. The sword would cut them down. The enemy would come to destroy. The enemy would be like the grasshopper or locust that devours everything in its path, leaving nothing behind (verse 15).

In Nahum's day Nineveh was a prosperous city filled with merchants. These merchants, however, were like the locust. Their only interest was in what they could get for themselves. They came, they took everything they could get, and then went somewhere else to do the same. They were not concerned about the people of their own land. They were only interested in profit and would flee in time of war.

Nineveh's soldiers were also compared to locusts and grasshoppers (verse 17). On a cold day, guards would sit on the wall to keep warm; but when the sun came out, they would find a more comfortable position. They were not dependable. They protected their people when it was convenient; but in the heat of battle, they abandoned their posts.

In the last two verses, Nahum directly addresses the king of Assyria. Nahum reports that Assyria's leaders were asleep (verse 18). There was no one to care for the people. The nobles themselves had lain down to rest, weary of the battle. While the leaders and nobles slept, the people were being scattered on the mountains and left to fend for themselves.

Nothing would heal Nineveh's wound. It was a fatal wound. Assyria's end had come. Nothing could be done to save her now. No one felt compassion for her. Instead, the nations she had oppressed would clap their hands and rejoice at her death. They had all felt her cruelty.

We see from all this that the Lord is a God of judgment and anger. This prophecy of Nahum shows us clearly that the Lord God will one day judge the earth even as he judged the nation of Assyria. Maybe you have friends and relatives who will experience this terrible judgment of the Lord. While he is a God of love and forgiveness, he is also a God of wrath and terror. How important it is for us to understand what Nahum tells us in chapter 1:

> The LORD is good,
> a refuge in times of trouble.
> He cares for those who trust in him,
> but with an overwhelming flood
> he will make an end of [Nineveh];
> he will pursue his foes into darkness. (Nahum 1:7–8)

The prophecy of Nahum calls us all to make a decision. Have we put our trust in the Lord as our only refuge? The warning of Nahum cannot be ignored. He paints a very graphic picture of the fury and wrath of God. As Nahum tells us: "He cares for those who trust in him, but with an overwhelming flood . . . he will pursue his foes into darkness" (Nahum 1:7–8). This is a warning we cannot afford to ignore.

For Consideration:

- What does this passage teach us about the danger of lust?

- Was God just in his judgment of Nineveh? Explain.

- Nahum asked Nineveh to look to the city of Thebes as an example of the judgment of God. What examples has God given us of his judgment?

- Why is it so important that we understand that God is a God of righteous anger?

For Prayer:

- Thank the Lord for the health and strength he has given you. Ask him to forgive you for the times that you have taken this for granted.

- Take a moment to pray for someone who does not really understand the fury and wrath of God against sin. Ask God to bring this person to himself.

- Thank God that although his wrath is real, through the Lord Jesus we have been rescued from that wrath.

- Ask the Lord to deliver you from the lust for pleasure, possessions, and power.

Habakkuk

13

Why?

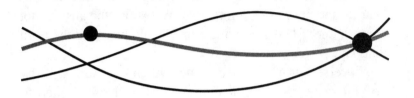

Read Habakkuk 1:1–17

Have you ever questioned the purposes of God? Are there not times in our lives when we simply do not understand why God does what he does? Habakkuk found himself in this situation. There were many things happening around him that he did not understand.

We know very little about Habakkuk. The only reference to his name in the Bible is here in this book. He prophesied at a time when the nation of Babylon was oppressing the people of God. Habakkuk saw the violence and injustice around him and wondered what God was doing. This chapter is full of questions to God about what was happening in his nation.

Notice in verse 1 that this prophecy is a word that the prophet Habakkuk received from the Lord. God brought him to a point of asking questions. Though the questions the prophet asked were really his, God ordained that he ask them for the sake of those who would receive his prophecy.

The prophecy opens with Habakkuk asking his first question. "How long, O LORD, must I call for help, but you do not listen? Or cry out to you, 'Violence!' but you do not save?" (verse 2). Have you ever wondered why God does not answer your prayers sooner? Even as I write, there is an issue on my heart that I have brought for years to the Lord. I have often wept over this issue in my prayers to God. Yet the matter seems to remain unchanged. Who among us has not been in this situation? We have the assurance from his Word that if what we ask is according to his will, he will hear us and answer (1 John 5:14). Why does the answer not come sooner? This is the question Habakkuk asked the Lord that day.

In verse 3 the prophet continues with his questions. "Why do you make me look at injustice?" Habakkuk wanted to know why the Lord tolerated the wickedness that abounded around him. Destruction and violence seemed to thrive. Contention and strife flourished. The law of God appeared to be paralyzed as men and women ignored it. That law did not seem to have any impact on the decisions that God's people made. Judah had no respect for the law of God. Justice never seemed to prevail. The wicked surrounded the righteous and the righteous were powerless against them. Why, God, why? You can feel the prophet's confusion.

Habakkuk's society was not unlike our own. He was grieved at how the people of his day had turned their backs on God and rejected his law. They openly perverted justice. They were a violent people who seemed to thrive on strife and conflict among themselves. The righteous were in the minority.

The Israelites were guilty of oppressing each other. God's people were mistreating their own brothers and sisters (Jeremiah 22:13–17). Habakkuk spoke to God about the state of his nation. He asked some very important questions. Why does injustice prevail? Why do the righteous have to suffer at the hands of the ungodly? Why do we continue to pray for justice and righteousness to prevail and God does not seem to answer? Why do people openly rebel against the law of God, and yet God allows them to continue to prosper? Why doesn't he break through and cause righteousness to triumph? Are these not questions we all ask?

The Lord responds in verse 5. "Look at the nations and watch—and be utterly amazed. For I am going to do something in your days that you would not believe, even if you were told." God is promising Habakkuk that the day will come when he will take his stand and indeed break through to bring justice.

Verse 6 tells us that God is going to raise up the Babylonians. These fierce people would become God's servants to judge those who were guilty before God. Through the Babylonians, God would judge his very own people for their sins.

Consider for a moment who these Babylonians were. Verses 6–11 describe them. They were a ruthless and impetuous people who did whatever they wanted (verse 6). They would sweep across the earth, seizing dwelling places that were not their own. On their military campaigns, they took whatever they wanted. They were a feared and dreaded people. They were a law unto themselves. They were subject to no one. Their only interest was to promote their own honor (verse 7). They would crush anything or anyone who stood in the way of obtaining what they wanted.

Babylonian horses were swifter than leopards (verse 8). They were fiercer than a hungry wolf at dusk seeking his prey (verse 8). Their cavalry galloped headlong—charging toward the enemy. Like vultures, they swooped down unnoticed to destroy their prey (verse 8).

The Babylonians were a people intent on violence. They advanced in great numbers. Like the wind in the desert, they swept through the land, gathering people like the sand (verse 9). Nothing could stand in their way. They gathered prisoners as effortlessly as the great wind picked up grains of sand as it blew through the desert.

This enemy did not fear or respect the kings of the earth (verse 10). They scoffed at world leaders. The Babylonians laughed at the fortified walls of their enemies' cities. They built ramps against these walls and broke through to destroy and capture the inhabitants hidden behind them (verse 10). They swept past their enemies like the wind (verse 11).

The Babylonians were a guilty and immoral people whose only god was their own strength (verse 11). The only thing they would respond to was brute strength and violence. They believed that they could have anything they wanted by force. They lived by the sword and very often died by the sword. They took what they wanted by show of strength. The strongest among them was the most respected and honored.

As Habakkuk is shown this vision of the invading army of the Babylonians, he asks yet another question: "LORD, are you not from everlasting?" (verse 12). What is he asking here? Habakkuk seems to be reminding himself that although the Babylonian army is very powerful, only God is from everlasting. He is a God who has no beginning. He is the creator of the ends of the earth. In light of what was going to happen in the land, it must have been encouraging to know that the Lord God was greater than the approaching enemy. Hidden in this question is the thought that since God is greater than the approaching Babylonian army, could he not stop them or do something about them for the sake of his people?

"My God, my Holy One," Habakkuk writes, "we will not die" (verse 12). Although the enemy surrounded them and was intent on violence, God the Holy One would do what was right. Although many people in Israel would have to die because of their sin, God would remember his promises to his people. Israel would not be exterminated. God would always allow a remnant to remain to carry on his plan and purposes for Israel. Notice here how the prophet clings to the holiness of God in this situation. As a holy God, he will always do what was right. Truth and righteousness will prevail.

"O LORD," continues Habakkuk, "you have appointed them to execute judgment." Here in this phrase, the prophet speaks about the lordship and sovereignty of God. He recognizes that the Lord God does as he pleases. He recognizes that God has chosen to use the ungodly Babylonians to judge his own sinful people. Habakkuk knows that his own people have not lived as God required. He understands that the sentence of God is just.

Notice also in this verse that Habakkuk calls God his Rock. "O Rock, you have ordained them to punish." Rock is often used in Scripture to speak of a refuge or shelter. God is a stronghold. He is an unfailing and changeless rock and shelter in the time of difficulty. Habakkuk realized that even though the Lord God, the Holy One, had determined to punish his guilty people, they would still be safe in him. He would be their rock and shelter in the time of discipline.

How important it is for us to understand these things in our own time of trouble. When things are not turning out as we would like, we need to realize that God is a holy God. He will do what is right. As Lord, he is in absolute control of our circumstances. He is the Rock and will always be our refuge and protection in the storms we face. While the prophet did not understand the ways of God, he was encouraged by who God is.

Habakkuk did not have an answer to his questions, but he did see the one who was working out his purposes. Little children are often like this. Their minds are not able to understand the complex problems of life, but they are able to place their confidence in us as adults. What a comfort it is for the children of God, in their time of confusion, just to know that God has not abandoned them. In his trial Habakkuk saw God and that made all the difference. Habakkuk did not understand what God was doing, but in his confusion he continued to strongly trust God.

In verse 13 Habakkuk wonders: "Your eyes are too pure to look on evil; you cannot tolerate wrong. Why then do you tolerate the treacherous? Why are you silent while the wicked swallow up those more righteous than themselves?" The prophet knew that God was allowing all these things to happen, but he was still perplexed. He knew that God would work these things out, but he didn't understand why God allowed such wickedness to happen in the first place. He trusted God, but did not understand his ways.

In verse 14 Habakkuk compares the poor and oppressed to fish in the sea. The strong cast a net into the sea and capture the weak. The strong pull the weak out with hooks; they gather their catch in dragnets and rejoice. There was terrible injustice all around. Habakkuk believed God but did not understand why the wicked oppressed the poor without God immediately intervening.

Habakkuk tells us in verse 16 that the Babylonians worshiped their nets. Do these nets represent their military might and strength? Earlier in this chapter, Habakkuk told us that the Babylonians worshiped their own strength. Their strength was in their army. They worshiped their military power. They worshiped their gods of war. Why would this ungodly nation, which did not bow the knee to the one true sovereign Lord, be allowed to defeat God's people? How long would God allow these ungodly Babylonians to continue throwing out their nets of oppression and affliction? (verse 17).

Habakkuk asks some very important questions in this chapter. We have the distinct impression that while he did not receive clear answers to these questions, he did not doubt for a moment that his God was in control. There are times when we too do not have all the answers. In the midst of all these difficult questions, Habakkuk reminds us that God is still the Holy One. He is still LORD. He is still our Rock. Though we do not understand, we can place our confidence in him.

For Consideration:

• Have you ever asked yourself some of the questions that Habakkuk asked here in this chapter? What in particular caused you to ask these questions?

• What particular comfort do you find in verse 12 where Habakkuk reminds us that God is the Holy One and our Rock?

• What particular question do you have for God right now? How does this chapter help you?

For Prayer:

• Thank the Lord that he is still in control of this world.

• Ask him to give you strength to trust him despite the fact that you do not have all the answers right now.

• Commit your particular problem to him and ask him to give you patience to wait on him in it.

14

God Will Judge

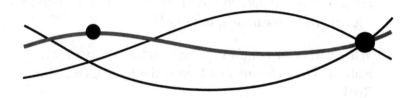

Read Habakkuk 2:1–20

In the last chapter, we heard the questions that Habakkuk asked God. Those questions related to why the Lord allowed violence and injustice to continue in the land and why the Lord allowed an idolatrous and lawless people to oppress his children. In this chapter the prophet is reassured that justice will be done.

Habakkuk begins chapter 2 by stating that he has stationed himself on the ramparts to take his watch. Habakkuk is waiting for the response of the Lord to his questions. The prophet's ears and eyes are as alert as a city guard to what God will say in response to his questions.

Habakkuk had asked God his questions. Now all he could do was wait. There is a time to ask and there is also a time to wait. Sometimes our persistence in asking is an indication of a lack of faith. We may continue to ask because we wonder if God has really heard us. We continue to ask just in case we did not ask correctly the last time. It sometimes takes more faith to stop asking for things we have already brought to the Lord. There is a time to continue asking, but there is also a time to stop asking and simply wait.

There have been times when I have seen God answer prayers that I had forgotten I prayed. Habakkuk had prayed. God had heard his request. Now Habakkuk waited in faith for him to answer.

The Lord did not remain silent. In verse 2 he speaks to Habakkuk, telling him to write down on tablets the things he is about to hear so that a courier can run with the message. The idea here is that God's message was to be written down so that messengers could take it and share it with the people of God wherever they went.

The vision or revelation that God was to give his prophet Habakkuk would see its fulfillment in time (verse 3). Though the fulfillment lingered, it would come to pass. God's people were to wait expectantly for its fulfillment. They were not to lose hope. The day would come when there would be an end of violence and despair.

God was not blind to those who oppressed his people. God saw the Babylonians as a proud, puffed up, and unrighteous people. He knew the arrogance and pride of their hearts. He saw the violence and immorality.

God calls his people to live by faith at all times (verse 4). Habakkuk 2:4 is an important verse. This passage is quoted three times in the New Testament (Romans 1:17; Galatians 3:11; Hebrews 10:38). This repetition indicates that this principle was vital not only for the people of Habakkuk's day but for us as well. It should be noted that at the time Habakkuk spoke these words, things were very difficult. God's people were suffering and there was injustice all around them. It was at this time that faith was necessary. God's people were to wait on him in confidence and trust.

Sometime ago I purchased a product over the Internet. While the product was paid for and in the mail, I did not have it in my hand. I knew it was mine though I had never seen it or handled it. I remember at that time bringing a particular request to the Lord in prayer. I wrestled for some time with this request. One day as I was sitting on a rock in the woods, I wrestled with God over this matter. The Lord reminded me of that parcel in the mail. He made it clear to me that he had heard my request and that the answer too was in the mail. I only had to wait for its arrival. In faith that day, I accepted what God said. I found tremendous liberty in this. This is what the Lord told Habakkuk that day. God knew the arrogance and ungodliness of the enemy that surrounded them. The Lord would come to rescue his people in time. For now they were to wait on that answer.

In verse 5 God tells Habakkuk that wine betrayed the enemy. The enemy was intoxicated with the wine of pleasure and lust. The Babylonians were drunk with the wine of greed and materialism. They filled themselves with the wine of ungodliness. Even as the drunkard never seems to have enough wine, so the Babylonians were greedy for more pleasure, possessions, and power. They were as greedy as the grave. Like death that never seems to have enough victims, so this foe continued to take more and more captives and possessions. God knew the heart of the enemy and saw his deeds.

God reminds Habakkuk in verses 6–13 that he will judge the enemy for his violence, injustice, and greed. The day was coming when Babylon, the oppressor, would be the object of scorn and ridicule. Those whom Babylon had oppressed would one day ridicule this nation.

The Babylonians had piled up stolen objects. They had made themselves wealthy by extortion. They had taken by force what was not theirs. The day was coming when their debtors would rise up against them. The captives would wake up and take a stand against their oppressor. The captives would give Babylon cause to tremble in their presence. The oppressor would become the victim of the oppressed (verse 7).

Babylon had plundered many nations, but soon they would be plundered (verse 8). They would be looted because they had destroyed lands and cities and everyone in them. They had built up their realm by unjust gain (verse 9). They had thought they were safe and that nothing could touch them. To their own shame, they had plotted to ruin many people. In so doing they had sealed their destiny—they forfeited their own lives (verse 10). The stones in the walls of the cities they had built through bloodshed would cry out to God against them. The beams of the houses they had built through bloodshed would echo the same cry (verse 11).

"Woe to him who builds a city with bloodshed and establishes a town by crime," says the Lord (verse 12). All things obtained through crime will become as fuel for the fire. God is saying that unjust people exhaust themselves for nothing. In the end they do not prosper. Their own injustice, greed, and violence will destroy them. The prophet Habakkuk reminds us here that the foundation we build on is of utmost importance. If we build our lives on injustice, greed, and violence, we will surely fall. For a time we may prosper, but our fall is sure.

The day is coming, writes Habakkuk, when the whole earth will be filled with the knowledge of the glory of God, as the waters cover the sea (verse 14). God will not allow the ungodly to prosper forever. He will fill this earth with the knowledge of his glory. For some, that will be a day of terror. For those of us who love the Lord, however, it will be a wonderful day. Do not fear. Evil will not prevail. God will break through. His glory will be revealed. What a wonderful hope this gives us as we look at a world of injustice and greed. Our Lord will destroy this evil. The whole earth will know his glory and bow down to him as Lord.

Habakkuk has spoken about greed, injustice, and

violence. He now moves on to speak about the immorality and ungodliness in his land: "Woe to him who gives drink to his neighbors, . . . so that he can gaze on their nakedness" (verse 15). The prophet speaks here against the immoral lifestyles of his day. Things have not really changed in our day. Drunkenness and sexual immorality still exist. Immorality is promoted through television, literature, and movies. Our society has become obsessed with alcohol and sex. These too, warned Habakkuk, will be judged. Immoral people will be filled with shame instead of glory, as God makes them drink from the cup of his wrath and exposes them for what they are (verse 16). They will be disgraced and ashamed.

What would it take for our society to become ashamed of its immorality? A society that does not deal with its immorality cannot be a glorious society. Disgrace will cover such a society. The same thing is true of the life of the individual caught in this trap. The glory of God will not rest on the life of the person who chooses to live in immorality. Ask yourself what any society or any life would be like without the glory of God revealed in it. It would be a situation of despair and hopelessness. Though for the moment lusts are satisfied, this does not last. Soon the person is left empty and dry.

In verse 17 Habakkuk denounces Babylon for her cruelty and thoughtlessness toward God's people and land. Habakkuk has already spoken about the violence he saw all around him (1:2–17). Notice here that Babylon was also accused of destroying the land of Lebanon. God reminds the Babylonians that the violence they did to the land would come back on them. Not only had they shed human blood, but they also senselessly killed the animals and destroyed the environment as well (verse 17). We are not told how this happened, but these things did not go unnoticed. The anger and wrath of God would come as floodwaters on the Babylonians because of what they had done.

Are we too not reaping the results of our own disrespect for the environment God has given us? How may diseases and health problems in our day have their sources in our disrespect and destruction of the environment? Are we experiencing a similar judgment in our day?

Verse 18 and 19 condemn the idolatry of the land of Babylon. In chapter 1 we saw that the Babylonians had been worshiping their own strength. Power had become their idol. There are many things that societies lift up as idols. God reminded Habakkuk of the uselessness of these false gods. An idol is a human creation. People fashion idols and then lift them up to worship. Idol-makers believe the lie that an object of their own creation can help them. Idols cannot speak or reason. They are powerless, yet people bow the knee to them. We too can create idols of materialism or pleasure. Whatever takes us away from God and his Word can become an idol for us.

As Habakkuk prophesied about Babylon's destruction, he was also warning his own people about greed and materialism, about immorality and the destruction of the environment, and about idolatry. He challenged his own people to live righteous lives. He reminded them that there is only one God. He is holy and lives in his holy temple (verse 20).

We are commanded here to be silent before this Lord (verse 20). This silence is a silence of awe and reverence. It is a silence of confidence and respect. All other gods are powerless. There is only one true God. Our hope is in him alone. In the midst of all the confusion and unanswered questions of life, Habakkuk calls us to be silent before a holy and awesome God. He is in control. He will do what is right. We must wait on him in faith and confidence.

As we look at this chapter, the Lord does indeed provide

us with some answers to the perplexing questions of chapter 1. He reminds us that justice will be done. He reminds us that those who build on a foundation of oppression, greed, and lust build on a very shaky foundation. It will not be long before that foundation is destroyed. The day is coming when the glory of God will be revealed. We are called to wait in faith and confidence. He will reveal his glory in his time.

For Consideration:

- In what way could it be said that continually asking God for the same request could be a sign of weakness in faith? Can we know that God has heard us? When do we continue to pray and when do we simply wait in confidence?

- Consider what the prophet Habakkuk said about injustice, greed, immorality, destruction of the environment, and idolatry. How much of this is still relevant to our society today?

- Why do we feel the need to have immediate answers to our prayers?

For Prayer:

- Thank the Lord that he is in control.

- Take a moment to pray that God would open the eyes of the people in your town or city to the shaky foundation they may be building on.

- Ask God to increase your faith and confidence in him. Thank him that he has not abandoned you in your troubles. Thank him that he will come to your aid in his time.

- Ask God to teach you the lessons you need to learn in your time of trial.

15

A Song of Praise to God

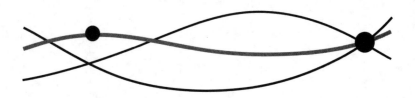

Read Habakkuk 3:1–19

The prophet began in chapter 1 by asking some important questions about suffering and justice. In the second chapter, the Lord reminded Habakkuk that he was a God of righteousness and justice, and the wicked would be judged. Here in this concluding chapter, the prophet records a song of praise to God.

Chapter 3 is a prayer in musical form. Commentators are uncertain as to the meaning of the word *shigionoth* found here in verse 1. It is likely a musical term depicting a certain form of music or Psalm.

Habakkuk opens this final chapter by calling on God to come and renew his deeds. Remember that the days in which Habakkuk lived were difficult days. The enemy had surrounded the righteous on all sides. This was a day in which evil seemed to prevail. Habakkuk remembered, however, that the God of Israel was an all-powerful and awesome God. Habakkuk had heard of the incredible things God had done in the past for his people.

All these deeds were wonderful but distant. They were the experiences of Habakkuk's ancestors and not his personal experiences. The prophet called on God to revive these experiences in his day. He asked God to descend and deal with the present situation as he had done in the past. In chapter 2 Habakkuk was given the assurance that God would come. Now the prophet asks God to be true to his word.

While Habakkuk wanted to see God repeat his wonderful works of judging evil and saving the righteous, he did have a request to make: "In wrath remember mercy" (verse 2). We need to remember that God is a God of holiness. We are sinners who fall short of the standard that he has set for us. Who could stand in the presence of such a show of holy justice unless it was tempered with compassion and mercy?

How we need to pray this prayer in our day as well. "O God, come and renew your works in our day. Reveal your power and your glory again in the eyes of my church, my city, and my nation. Come and show us your awesome deeds. As you come, however, remember that we are sinners, and show mercy and compassion on us." This is a cry for renewal and revival.

Even as Habakkuk prayed, he saw a vision of God coming in power. God came from Teman and Mount Paran. There is some difficulty understanding why God came from these particular locations. They were both located in the territory of Edom. We are uncertain why these two locations are mentioned here in this context. What is important is that God would come and reveal himself in the presence of his enemies. His glory would cover the heavens, and the earth would be filled with praise for the wonder of his character (verse 3).

Habakkuk compares God's splendor to the sunrise, an awesome thing to behold. Rays flashed from his hand where his power was hidden. There can be no doubt that as these rays of judgment left the hands of the Lord, the earth was filled with terror. Plagues went before him and pestilence followed his steps (verse 5).

When God stood, he shook the earth. He looked and the nations trembled. As powerful as the nations were, they knew that they were no match for this great and powerful God. Ancient mountains crumbled. Age-old hills collapsed in his presence. These mountains and hills had been around since the creation of the earth. They had endured the test of time. For centuries the winds and storms had beaten them and still they remained. They appeared to be ageless and indestructible; yet in the presence of holiness, they collapsed like a house of cards.

At the sight of God, the nations were in despair. There was terror among the tents of Cush. The dwelling places of Midian were in anguish. They were no match for such an awesome God. The day is coming when those who see him will hide in the mountains and hills, calling on the rocks to hide them from the wrath of this all-powerful and holy God (Revelation 6:16).

Habakkuk asks: "Were you angry with the rivers, O LORD? Was your wrath against the streams? Did you rage against the sea?" (verse 8). The prophet pictures the Lord riding with his horses and victorious chariots, striking the sea and the rivers. The Lord uncovers his bow and calls for his arrows. He shoots his arrows and splits the earth open with rivers. As from an open wound, the earth pours out her lifeblood, sapping her strength and vitality.

The mountains see the Lord and they writhe in agony. Torrents of water rise up and sweep by in a furious rage. The deep ocean roars and lifts up its waves (verse 10). The sun and the moon stand still in the heavens when they see the flashing of the Lord's arrows and the lightning of his swinging spear. In wrath the Lord rides throughout the earth and threshes the nations. No one can stand before him. Habakkuk's vision is very intense.

Notice in verse 13 the reason for this judgment and awesome show of power. God came to deliver his people and to save his anointed one. God's jealousy had been stirred. He lashed out against those who held his people under oppression and injustice. God crushed the leaders of this wickedness. He stripped them from head to toe because of what they were doing to his people. He pierced the head of his enemies with his spear, destroying them. He did this because they had stormed out against his people, gloating as they devoured them. He trampled the sea and churned up the waters because of his jealousy for his people.

What words of comfort these must have been to a people surrounded by the enemy. The Lord had not abandoned them in their hour of need. He rose up in furious jealousy. He struck out against those who had harmed his people. Such was his love for them.

When Habakkuk heard these things, his heart pounded. His lips quivered at the sound of the coming judgment. Decay crept into his bones and his legs trembled at the thought of what was about to happen. In light of what he heard from God, Habakkuk makes a personal commitment (verses 17–18).

Before God that day the prophet promised that even though the fig tree did not bud and there were no grapes on the vine, he would still rejoice in the Lord. Though there was no food in the fields and the sheep pen and cattle stall were empty, he would choose still to rejoice in the Lord. Notice here that he makes this choice in light of the clear teaching of the Word of the Lord. Habakkuk, despite what was happening around him, chose to rejoice in the Lord and be joyful in God his Savior.

Notice that he calls God his Savior. A Savior is one who saves. For Habakkuk the victory was already won. He could rejoice and be joyful because he knew the Lord would give him victory.

There is a decision for each of us to make. Will we rejoice and be glad in our Savior or will we doubt and give the enemy the victory in our lives? How many of us live as through the enemy is stronger than God himself. Hasn't God promised us the victory? Will he not be true to his Word? Is this not reason to rejoice?

Not only is joy and rejoicing a fruit of the Spirit, it is a choice on our part. When the enemy surrounds us as they surrounded God's people in the days of Habakkuk, we too can choose to believe the Word of God and live in the joy of the victory. The temptation is to look at the difficulties rather than at the One who promises victory.

We may ask how it is possible to rejoice in our trials. Habakkuk concludes his writings by telling us that the Lord will make our feet as strong as the deer. He will enable us to go up to the heights. Right now, you may be in the depth of despair because of your circumstances. God is your strength. He can bring you up out from that pit and give you strong legs like the deer to climb to the heights of joy and rejoicing. Will you take that strength he offers? Will you make a conscious decision to rejoice and be joyful in your Savior?

The enemy delights in causing us to question the purposes of God. He delights to see us live as if there were no victory in sight. Habakkuk had lots of questions. He wondered why the righteous had to suffer. God did not give him an answer to this question. What God did, however, was reveal himself to the prophet. He revealed himself as the God of justice and holiness. He showed himself to Habakkuk as God the Savior. That was enough. Habakkuk realized that he did not need to have the answers to the questions of pain and suffering. All he needed to know was that God was over it all and would work out his sovereign purposes in the end.

This book deals with the problem of pain and suffering

in the lives of the children of God. It asks some very deep questions. Habakkuk reminds us that there is no blessing in rebellion against God. Those who turn their backs on God choose a life of despair and defeat. God will bring justice in his time. Evil will not triumph. In the meantime, we are called to live by faith. We are called to trust that although the fig tree does not blossom for us right now, God will bring forth justice and blessing in his time. He will come to deliver his people. We can rejoice in this and trust him fully. We may not have the answers to our questions, but we can be absolutely confident in the Lord our God.

For Consideration:

- What evil surrounds us as a nation today? What evil surrounds you personally?

- What comfort do you take from this passage?

- Could it be said that despair in the life of a believer shows a lack of faith?

- What is the difference between weariness brought on by constant opposition and weariness brought on by despair?

- To what extent is contentment and joy a choice on our part?

For Prayer:

- Thank God that he has promised us victory over our enemies.

- Ask the Lord to make you willing to choose life and rejoicing over despair.

- Are there some people in your life who are being surrounded by the enemy even now? Take a moment to pray that the Lord would minister to them.

Zephaniah

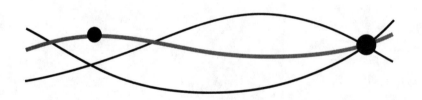

16

Complacency

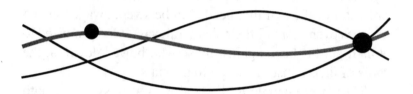

Read Zephaniah 1:1–18

This is the prophecy of Zephaniah. Verse 1 tells us that he was a prophet during the reign of Josiah. This places him at a time prior to the exile of the nation of Judah. Josiah sought to return the nation to the Lord. The reforms that took place during his reign, however, would not last. The people would quickly return to their evil ways. From the first chapter of this prophecy, we see that God was angry because of the impurity he saw in the land.

The Lord told his people through Zephaniah that he would sweep away everything from the earth (verse 2). As God looked on the land, he saw that it was in desperate need of cleansing. God was going to take out his broom and sweep away the dirt of sin and evil.

Notice the extent of sin and filth in the land (verse 3). Its cleansing would affect people, animals, birds, and fish. The wicked would be left with only heaps of rubble. That is to say, God would reduce them to a pile of rubble.

Notice that this judgment was against the people of Judah. This was the nation that God had chosen to honor and glorify his name. Here in this nation, his name was to be lifted high. Instead, there was tremendous evil. Notice what the Lord discovered in the land of Judah.

Verse 4 tells us that in the city where the Lord's name was to be honored, the Lord had to destroy every detail of Baal worship and the names of his pagan and idolatrous priests. Right in the city of Jerusalem were individuals who had bowed the knee to the foreign god Baal. This was only part of the evil that needed to be swept away. Verse 5 exposes even more of their shameful ways. God promised to stretch out his hand against those who bowed down on the roofs of their houses to worship the stars.

There were people in the land who were swearing both in the name of the Lord and also in the name of Molech. The people were mixing their faith in the Lord God with the practices of idolatry from foreign lands. Judah no longer sought the Lord or inquired of the one true God. These things too would be swept clean by the broom of God's holy judgment.

We cannot lightly pass over these accusations. Those who practiced these things were the inhabitants of Jerusalem, the people of God. God's own people had found other lovers. They bowed down to other gods and worshiped the stars. What other gods are there in our churches today? The gods of materialism, lust, and reason are all very much alive today. Are there believers in our churches today who consult the horoscopes in their local newspaper? Are there believers who have not yet made a complete break from their old fleshly ways? Are we guilty of not consulting the Lord in the matters of our church and personal lives? Are the sins of Judah being repeated in our day?

Zephaniah called the nation to be silent before the Lord (verse 7). This was a silence of reflection and anticipation.

It was a silence of one who awaits the judgment of the Lord. Zephaniah prophesied that the day of the Lord was near. The day was coming when the Lord would prepare a sacrifice and consecrate those he invited. Judah would be set aside as this sacrifice.

What a dreadful day that day of sacrifice would be. On that day the Lord would punish Judah's princes, the king's sons, and those dressed in foreign clothes. These princes and king's sons were the leaders of the people. They should have led God's people into the praise and worship of the Lord, but they didn't. Those wearing foreign clothes could possibly refer to those who wore robes associated with Baal worship or some other form of foreign worship and practice. These religious leaders were directing God's people away from him. God's wrath would fall on them too.

On that day of sacrifice, God would punish everyone who avoided stepping on the threshold and who filled the temple of their foreign gods with violence and deceit (verse 9). The practice of not stepping on the threshold could refer to the idol worship of the Philistines, as referred to in 1 Samuel 5. This passage reveals that the Philistines placed the Ark of the Covenant in the temple of Dagon. In the morning when they came to the temple, the statue of Dagon had fallen on its face before the Ark of the Covenant. Dagon's head and hands had broken off and were lying on the threshold. 1 Samuel 5:5 tells us: "That is why to this day neither the priests of Dagon nor any others who enter Dagon's temple at Ashdod step on the threshold." Could it be that the people of Judah had adopted this pagan practice?

In the day of this great sacrifice, a great cry would go up from the Fish Gate. Wailing would be heard from the New Quarter and a loud crash in the hills surrounding the city (verse 10). The picture here is one of distress. The Lord would execute his judgment on the nation.

Zephaniah called the people of the market district to wail

because of this great judgment (verse 11). Those who traded with silver would be wiped out and be no more. Their sin and rebellion against God would bring God's anger on them.

So extensive would be the cleansing of the land that God told them that he would search it with lamps (verse 12). The idea here is that these lamps would shine into the dark corners where people were trying to hide. No one would escape this great judgment of God on the land.

God was going to punish those who were complacent (verse 12). These were individuals who had seen the evil that was happening in the land but had done nothing to stop it. These individuals were like wine left with its dregs. When the grapes were crushed, the juice was poured from one vessel to another to separate the good wine from the dregs that remained after the crushing. If the wine was left with the dregs, it spoiled the taste of the wine. This, said Zephaniah, was what the complacency of God's people was like. If they did not see to it that the sin and evil was removed, their whole society would be ruined. Similarly, Jesus told us that as believers we are the salt of the earth (Matthew 5:13). We have a preserving influence on our society. We are also told that we are to let our light shine in this world to preserve it from darkness (Matthew 5:14–16). The people of Judah in Zephaniah's day had left their society in its sin and decay. They had done nothing to preserve it. They said to themselves: "The LORD will do nothing either good or bad" (verse 12). They saw the Lord as being distant and complacent. They did not feel that God was concerned about their sin. They had no burden for the glory of the Lord.

God was angry with the believers who did not speak out about the sin in their land.

Because they were silent about sin, their wealth would be plundered (verse 13). Their houses would be demolished. They would build houses but not be able to live in them. They would plant vineyards but not be able to drink the wine. Others would enjoy the proceeds of their hard work. The blessing of God would be removed from their lives.

Have we developed this sort of complacency in our day as well? Do we see the evil that is going on around us but do nothing about it? Do we sit in front of our televisions and allow the evil influences of the media to shape our minds and the minds of our children? Do we refuse to stand up for what is right and godly in our land? Will God not judge our land for this? What about our churches? As church leaders, are we so afraid of losing people in our congregations that we prefer to tolerate their evil rather than speak out against it. Zephaniah paints a picture of God's people steeped in sin and no one doing anything about it. Everyone was saying that God wouldn't judge or take action. Have we been doing the same?

In verse 14 Zephaniah reminds his people that the day of the Lord is near. It is coming very quickly. That day would come much sooner than they realized. It would be a day of tremendous bitterness. On that day they would hear the cry of the warrior. So great would be the pain and despair that even the mightiest warrior would be reduced to tears.

The day of God's wrath and judgment would be a day of great distress and anguish (verse 15). It would be a day of trouble and pain, darkness and gloom, and clouds and blackness. It would be a day of trumpet sounds and battle cries. God would unleash his anger against the fortified cities and the strong towers of the land. Nothing would stand in his way.

On the day of his judgment, God would bring distress on his sinful people. They would walk in blindness, not knowing where they were going. God would remove his presence and they would have no direction or guidance. Because they had sinned against the Lord, their blood would be poured out like dust (verse 17). In other words, their blood would be considered as useless as the dust of the earth.

Their silver and their gold would not protect them on that day of wrath. In his jealousy and righteous anger, the Lord would sweep them clean. He would cleanse the earth of their presence. He would consume the sin and rebellion in the fire of his great justice and holiness. He would make a sudden end of all who lived in the land.

God's people had been guilty of complacency. They had embraced the foreign, ungodly influences of the nations around them. They had accepted these abominable practices and done nothing about evil in their land. God decided that it was time to do major house cleaning. He took up his broom of justice and holiness and began the process of cleansing the evil from his land. He spared nothing in the process.

For Consideration:

- What would God find in our land if he were to come to judge it today? What would he find in our churches or in our personal lives?

- What influences of the world have crept into the church today?

- To what extent are we guilty of complacency in our day?

- What does the Lord teach us here in this passage about the sin of complacency?

For Prayer:

- Thank the Lord that he cares enough for his work that he will take the effort to cleanse it.

- Ask the Lord to reveal to you any way in which you have been guilty of complacency or indifference to the sin around you.

- Ask the Lord to show you what you can do to be part of the solution to the problem in our churches and society today.

17

The Remnant

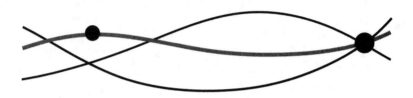

Read Zephaniah 2:1–15

In the last chapter we saw that the Lord was going to do major house cleaning in the land of Judah. The nation of Judah was guilty before the Lord. God was going to deal with her sin and cleanse the land.

Here in this second chapter, the Lord commands his people to gather together (verse 1). Judah had become a shameless nation. God's people felt no disgrace for their sins. Why did God call them to come together? Verse 2 leads us to believe that it had something to do with the judgment that was coming on the land. They were to come together before they were blown away like chaff. They were to come together before the fierce anger of the Lord came on them. They were to gather together in light of Zephaniah's prediction of judgment in chapter 1.

Verse 3 goes on to announce that when God's people gathered, they were to seek the Lord. They were to humble themselves, turn from their evil ways, and seek God's righteousness. Zephaniah challenges them to seek God with all their hearts and souls. This is a very serious matter. God is not interested in an external show of emotion and religion. He is interested in their hearts and their sincerity. They are to seek him so that perhaps in the day of his fierce anger, they might be sheltered.

What is important for us to understand here is that God is a God of justice and wrath. He is also, however, a God of compassion and forgiveness. Zephaniah is telling Judah that God is willing to offer forgiveness and compassion to those who will confess their sins, humble themselves, and seek God's face. Even though judgment has been proclaimed, there is still time to be reconciled with God. It is not too late. Similarly, if there are things that need to be made right in your life, don't waste another moment. Humble yourself and seek God's righteousness. Perhaps he will shelter you too with his wings of forgiveness.

In the verses that follow, Zephaniah prophesies what will happen to the nations who had oppressed the children of God. Chapter 1 reminded Judah that her people had fallen short of God's standard. Despite this, God still clearly loved them. He also saw what the ungodly nations had been doing to his chosen ones. He would not allow this to continue. Even though Judah had sinned, God would not abandon her in his judgment of her.

God addresses four principle enemies of his children in this passage. He begins in verses 4–7 by speaking to the Philistine nation.

Philistia (verses 4–7)

Four cities of the Philistines are mentioned in these verses. Gaza would be abandoned. Ashkelon would be left in ruins. Ashdod would be emptied. Ekron would be uprooted. All these principle Philistine cities were to be destroyed.

The Philistines had been a source of tremendous

oppression to God's people. From the time of David, they were one of the principle enemies of God's people. God knew what they had done to his people. Though his own children were not always faithful to him, God would, nonetheless, defend their cause. Philistia would know the anger of the Lord: "Woe to you who live by the sea," announced the Lord (verse 5). Philistia was located on the seacoast. "O Kerethite people," prophesied Zephaniah, "the word of the Lord is against you." Commentators tell us that the term "Kerethite" comes from the early geographical origins of the Philistine nation. It is another name used for the Philistines. Ezekiel used this same name for the Philistines in Ezekiel 25:15–16: "This is what the Sovereign LORD says: 'Because the Philistines acted in vengeance and took revenge with malice in their hearts, and with ancient hostility sought to destroy Judah, therefore this is what the Sovereign Lord says: I am about to stretch out my hand against the Philistines, and I will cut off the Kerethites and destroy those remaining along the coast.'"

The Lord was against the Kerethite people. He would destroy Canaan, the land of the Philistines so that no one would be left in the land. The Canaanites were in the land prior to the coming of the Philistines who took over the coastal region of Canaan.

This land by the sea where these Kerethite (Philistine) people lived would one day become a place for shepherding sheep (verse 6). The land of the Philistines would be handed over to the remnant of the house of Judah. There in this land, Judah would shepherd her sheep. In the evening these sheep would sleep in the houses of Ashkelon, one of the principle cities of the Philistines. Philistia would be left in ruins and her land given to Judah.

Moab and Ammon (verses 8–11)
The Lord shifts his attention to the territory of the

Moabites and the Ammonites. "I have heard the insults of Moab and the taunts of the Ammonites," says the Lord (verse 8). Obviously, they had insulted the people of God and made threats against their land. While the Ammonites and the Moabites were not so much a physical threat to the children of God, they were still their enemies. Their weapon against God's people here was their tongue. How important it is that we understand that our words can also wound. You may never physically strike your enemy, but your words can do more damage than any broken bone or wounded flesh.

God was aware of the things that were being said against his people. How careful we need to be in what we say about the children of God. Listen to the judgment of God on the Moabites and the Ammonites because of the words spoken against his children.

Moab would become like Sodom. Ammon would become like Gomorrah. Both of these cities were completely destroyed by fire from heaven in the days of Abraham and Lot. Moab and Ammon would become places of weeds and salt pits where nothing could grow. Their territories would become a wasteland forever. God's children would plunder them and inherit their lands. God would judge Moab and Ammon because of their pride and because they had insulted and mocked the children of the Lord Almighty. God would show his awesome power in favor of his people. The nations all around would see his awesome deeds and bow down to the God of Israel.

We see here how serious it is to mock and insult one of God's children. How often we carelessly say things about the children of God. Zephaniah warns us that we must be very careful in this matter. This passage is a real challenge to us too.

Cush (verse 12)

The next people to be addressed are the Cushites. Cush

was the land of the Ethiopians and the Egyptians. The Egyptians in particular had been a threat and temptation to the people of God. Zephaniah simply tells us here that they would be slain by the sword.

Assyria (verses 13–15)

The final nation addressed is the nation of Assyria (verses 13–15). God would stretch out his hand against the north and destroy the land of the Assyrians. Nineveh, the capital city, would be desolate and dry like the desert. Flocks and herds would lie down in what was a once prosperous city. Creatures of every kind would roam through the streets. The desert owl would roost in Nineveh's columns and call through the windows of the abandoned buildings. Rubble would litter the doorways and the beams would be exposed. These once busy and prosperous buildings would lie abandoned. The once carefree city that lived in safety and security would be in ruins. The one who boasted of greatness by saying, "I am, and there is none besides me," would be scoffed. People passing by would shake their fists in anger and hatred. Assyria would fall, never to rise again.

It is important that we understand this chapter in light of chapter 1. In chapter 1 God very clearly spoke out against his own people. They had fallen short of his standard. They were complacent and unfaithful to their God. Here in this chapter, however, God takes up their defense against those who had mocked, insulted, oppressed, and wounded them. Though God's people were not always faithful, they were still his children.

It is very easy for us to feel free to speak out against God's people when they fall or do not see things the way we see them. This passage reminds us that God loves his children whether they are faithful to him or not. God will not abandon his loved ones. Even though we may be unfaithful to him, he remains faithful to us.

For Consideration:

- What does this passage teach us about God's love for his children?

- Have you ever been guilty of speaking out against one of God's children? What warning does this passage give you?

- What comfort do you find in the fact that God's love for you does not depend on how good you are?

For Prayer:

- Thank the Lord that his love for us does not change with our faithfulness or unfaithfulness.

- Do you know believers who have wandered in their spiritual lives? Ask the Lord what he would have you to do for them in this time of wandering.

- Ask God to forgive you for the things you have said about other believers who have not seen things as you do. Ask him to teach you to love them as he loves them.

18

Renewal in the City

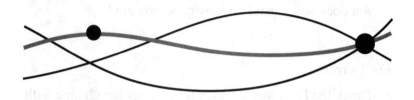

Read Zephaniah 3:1–20

I n the last chapter, Zephaniah spoke about the judgment of God on the nations that had oppressed Israel. Next he turns his attention to the people of God and their sin. The prophet addresses the city of Jerusalem, which represented all of God's people.

Zephaniah begins by reminding God's people that they were not right with him. In the last chapter, we saw how the Lord defended his people against their oppressors. We were reminded, however, that although God came to their defense, they were still far from perfect in their walk with him. They had many faults and sins that needed to be dealt with. God spoke of his people as a city of oppressors and rebels. They were defiled. They had rebelled. Repeatedly, the Lord sent prophets to correct them, but they refused to listen. They were guilty of oppressing each other. At times they even used their brothers and sisters as slaves. The city of Jerusalem was filled with sinners.

Zephaniah reminds the people of God that they obey no one. They reject correction. They do not trust the Lord. They refuse to draw near to God (verse 2). These are serious accusations.

Jerusalem's officials were like roaring lions. They walked about seeking prey to devour. These leaders used the people for their own ends. Jerusalem's rulers were like evening wolves. They came out in the evening when they would not be seen stalking their prey. By the time the morning came, they had cleaned up their prey and left nothing to be seen. They were dishonest and self-centered people.

The religious leaders were no better (verse 4). The false prophets were arrogant and treacherous men. They spoke their own hearts and not the heart of God. Their concern was not the Word of God but in getting people to like them. In this they were proud and arrogant. The priests were profaning the sanctuary and doing violence to the law of God. Their lifestyles left much to be desired. By serving with all their sin in the sanctuary, they were profaning the sanctuary. They did not respect the law of God but twisted it to suit their needs and desires.

Despite all the evil, the Lord, who dwelled in the midst of his people, was a righteous God who did no wrong. Morning by morning he dispensed his justice without fail. Unlike the religious and political leaders, he could not be corrupted. Everything he did was just and right. It is a wonder that the Lord remained among his people. Despite his righteous presence, the unrighteous still knew no shame and guilt for their actions.

In verses 6–8 God reminds his people that he will punish them for their shamelessness and sin. He reminds them of the nations that he had already cut off because of sin. He reminds them of how their strongholds had been demolished and their city streets deserted and destroyed, with no one left on them. In painting this picture, God reminds his people of how he had judged other nations. If he so judged other nations, would he hesitate to judge the city of Jerusalem and his own children when they had defiled it with evil?

"Surely you will fear me and accept correction," says the Lord. God did not delight in punishing his people. He would forgive them in an instant if they would only accept his correction and discipline. If they repented, they would not have to be punished. His people, however, were still eager to sin.

Because they refused to listen to him and correct their ways, God would stand up to testify against them for their actions. He would assemble the nations and gather the kingdoms of the earth to pour out his wrath and fierce anger on all of them. The whole earth would be consumed by the fire of his jealous anger. Sin would be judged. Oppression and opposition to his law would be crushed. God would come to judge. No one would escape.

Notice the result of this judgment of the earth in verses 9–13. The Lord will purify the lips of all the peoples (verse 9). Their lips will no longer be used to sin and speak out against the Lord. Instead their lips will call out to his name. The earth's peoples will serve the Lord God standing together, shoulder to shoulder. They will be unified in their effort to praise and serve the true and living God. While we are seeing this to a small degree through the work of the Lord Jesus in our day, it seems that the total fulfillment of this promise has yet to come.

God would do a powerful work of renewal and revival in the lives of his people. From beyond the rivers of Cush, God would gather his children to worship him. On that day they would have no cause for shame. God would renew their hearts. He would give them hearts that feared him and his laws.

God would remove from the city of Jerusalem all who rejoiced in their pride (verse 10–12). Never again would they be proud and arrogant on the holy hill of Jerusalem. Instead, they would be filled with praise and a humble recognition of their own shortcomings and sins. The only ones left in the once proud city of Jerusalem would be those who humbly trusted the Lord.

Those who were left after the judgment and renewal of God would do no wrong (verse 13). Their hearts would be devoted to the Lord their God. They would no longer speak lies; instead, they would live in the truth. Deceit would no longer be found in their mouths. The blessing of God would be on them. They would eat and lie down in safety. No one would make them afraid.

What a wonderful promise is given here to the people of God. They lived in an oppressive and rebellious nation that had been defiled. They did not obey God nor accept his correction. They refused to trust him and did not draw near to him. Their officials like roaring lions and evening wolves devouring their prey. Their religious leaders were arrogant and treacherous. They profaned the temple of God and did violence to his laws. It was into this situation that the Lord God would come. He would break through in judgment and pour out a spirit of humility and trust. God would not leave his people in their rebellion and wandering. He would visit them in power to renew the worship and praise of his name in their midst. How we need to see this in our day.

This was cause for great rejoicing in the land. The daughters of Zion were called to worship and shout out the praises of God with all their heart. "Be glad and rejoice," encourages Zephaniah in verse 14. The Lord had promised to renew and revive his people. He would not abandon them in their sin and rebellion. The Lord would take away their punishment and turn back their enemies. The Lord, the King of Israel, would be with them. They would never again need to fear harm. They had no need to be afraid, for God would come to them. No more would their hands hang limp at their sides, emptied of strength and vitality. They would be strengthened and renewed. In this they were to rejoice.

The Lord would be with them. He would be mighty to save them from all their enemies (verse 17). Who could come against them if the Lord was on their side? He would take great delight in them as his people. He would quiet them in his love, as a father holding his child to his breast. There in his love, they would be comforted and reassured. He would rejoice over them with singing. What a wonderful love this is. It is not that they deserved such love. Remember that God's people had been found guilty of great sin before him. Despite their sin, the love of their Father remained. I do not think I will ever understand how the Almighty God of this universe could ever have such deep and intimate feelings for a sinner like me, but I thank and praise him that he does.

The translation of verse 18 is somewhat difficult. The New International Version translates, "The sorrows for the appointed feasts I will remove from you; they are a burden and a reproach to you." This verse needs to be seen in its larger context. Verse 19 reminds us that the people of God had been scattered to various lands because of their sin. There in these foreign lands, the practice of these appointed feasts was not possible. They had sorrow because they were unable to practice these feasts as the Lord had commanded. The day was coming when the Lord would remove this shame and reproach. He would rescue from the hands of their enemies those who had been scattered and return them to a land where they could once again practice their appointed feasts. In those lands where they had been put to shame, the Lord would give them honor and praise. People would again look up to them as a glorious people.

From wherever they were scattered, God's people would again be returned to their land and enjoy the blessing of God. He would restore their fortunes and make them a glorious people. He would heal them and restore their health. How the church of our day needs to experience this renewal promised to the city of Jerusalem. How we again need to see the glory of the Lord restored to us as a church and as a people. What God promises to his people he can do for your church and for you as an individual.

For Consideration:

- Compare what God says about his people in verses 1–4 with what is happening in your own society today.

- What does this chapter teach us about the judgment of God and its purpose?

- What does verse 17 teach us about how God feels toward us as his people?

- Do believers need to see their glory restored today? How has the glory been diminished? Explain.

For Prayer:

- Thank the Lord for what this chapter reveals about how he feels toward us.

- Ask the Lord to restore our glory.

- Thank him that despite our sin and shortcomings, he does not abandon us as his people.

Endnotes

Chapter 11

[1]Nineveh was bordered by a series of rivers. These rivers acted as a barrier against attack from Nineveh's enemies. There was an ancient prophecy in Nineveh that stated that the city would not be overtaken until the river itself overtook it. History recounts that the Scythians tried unsuccessfully to overtake the city. After two years of unsuccessful attempts, one of those rivers swollen up with heavy rains took out part of the wall surrounding the city. Adam Clarke in his commentary on this passage quotes from an ancient account given by Diodorus Siculus:

> There was a prophecy received from their forefathers that Nineveh should not be taken till the river first became an enemy to the city. It happened in the third year of the siege, that the Euphrates (query, Tigris) being swollen with continued rains, overflowed part of the city, and threw down twenty stadia of the wall. The king then imagining that the oracle was accomplished, and that the river was now manifestly become an enemy to the city, casting aside all hope of safety, and lest he should fall into the hands of the enemy, built a large funeral pyre in the palace, and having collected all his gold and silver and royal vestments, together with his concubines and eunuchs, placed himself with them in a little apartment built in the pyre; burnt them, himself and the palace together. When the death of

the king (Sardanapalus) was announced by certain deserters, the enemy entered in by the breach which the waters had made, and took the city. (Clarke, Adam, *Adam Clarke's Commentary on the Bible*, Prepared for Bible Plus for Palm, version 2.99, public domain)

Light To My Path
Devotional Commentary Series

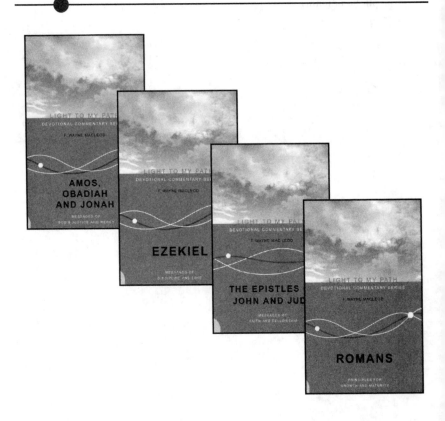

Now Available

Old Testament

- Ezra, Nehemiah, and Esther
- Ezekiel
- Amos, Obadiah, and Jonah
- Micah, Nahum, Habakkuk, and Zephaniah

New Testament

- John
- Acts
- Romans
- The Epistles of John and Jude

A new commentary series
for every day devotional use.

———————————————————●————————

"I am impressed by what I have read from this set of commentaries. I have found them to be concise, insightful, inspiring, practical and, above all, true to Scripture. Many will find them to be excellent resources."

Randy Alcorn
director of Eternal Perspective Ministries,
Author of *The Grace & Truth Paradox*
and *Money, Possessions & Eternity*

———————————————————●————————

Watch for more in the series
Spring 2005

Old Testament

- Israel
- Haggai, Zachariah and Malachi

New Testament

- Philippians and Colossians
- James and 1&2 Peter

Other books available from
Authentic Media . . .

Authentic
MEDIA

PO Box 1047
129 Mobilization Drive
Waynesboro, GA 30830

706-554-1594
1-8MORE-BOOKS
ordersusa@stl.org

Power of Generosity
How to Transform Yourself and Your World

David Toycen

An intimate journey down the road of giving, *The Power of Generosity* will strike a chord with all who want to fulfill a vital part of their humanity–the need to give.

Dave Toycen, President and CEO of World Vision Canada, believes generosity can save lives—both the benefactor's and the recipient's. The act of giving without an ulterior motive inherently nurtures a need human's have for significance. During three decades of traveling to the poorest and most desperate countries, Dave has seen and met individuals who have been freed by acts of generosity.

What is generosity? What motivates a person toward benevolence? *The Power of Generosity* is a practical guide to developing a spirit of generosity, providing thoughtful answers and encouragement for all those looking for ways to be more giving in their lives.

1-932805-10-9   192 Pages

Cat and Dog Theology
Rethinking Our Relationship With Our Master

Bob Sjogren & Dr. Gerald Robison

There is a joke about cats and dogs that conveys their differences perfectly.

> A dog says, "You pet me, you feed me, you shelter me, you love me, you must be God."
>
> A cat says, "You pet me, you feed me, you shelter me, you love me, I must be God."

These God-given traits of cats ("You exist to serve me") and dogs ("I exist to serve you") are often similar to the theological attitudes we have in our view of God and our relationship to Him. Using the differences between cats and dogs in a light-handed manner, the authors compel us to challenge our thinking in deep and profound ways. As you are drawn toward God and the desire to reflect His glory in your life, you will worship, view missions, and pray in a whole new way. This life-changing book will give you a new perspective and vision for God as you delight in the God who delights in you.

1-884543-17-0   206 Pages

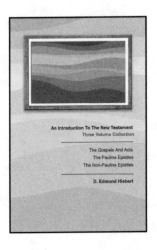

An Introduction To The New Testament
Three Volume Collection

D. Edmond Hiebert

Though not a commentary, the Introduction to the New Testament presents each book's message along with a discussion of such questions as authorship, composition, historical circumstances of their writing, issues of criticism and provides helpful, general information on their content and nature. The bibliographies and annotated book list are extremely helpful for pastors, teachers, and laymen as an excellent invitation to further careful exploration.

This book will be prized by all who have a desire to delve deeply into the New Testament writings.

Volume 1: The Gospels And Acts
Volume 2: The Pauline Epistles
Volume 3: The Non-Pauline Epistles and Revelation

1-884543-74-X   976 Pages